The Swan In The Orange Skirt

The Swan In The Orange Skirt

This is an essentially intimate, introspective, emblematic, vulnerable, and insightful memoir of an 18-year-old.

by

Olivia Walker

The Swan In The Orange Skirt

Hawk

Chilled metal poles compress handbags against exposed thighs and diaphanous fabric. Vodka-rose perfume and sole-pasted ginkgo leaves permeate the subway. Smoky, pigeon-blue seats caress the slim legs of a petite woman. The train halts and the parting doors hiss like the snake onyx and silver bands that emboss her ivory fingers. She hugs her body, mitigating the plague of agony and distress. She is subsisting without a Venetian mask, but she is using her own face as a swathe disguise.

Her raven, ink-lined, koi-pond eyes sharply scan furrowed faces. She observes a woman with hair bigger than her heart, and another with gypsy moths curled above Elizabeth Taylor lids. Her eyes wander over to the baby's leg hanging between hickory leather and cheetah prints. The wrinkles on a Kennedy coat mirror the waves separating lips of blood as shadows crawl around burnt-brick skin. People stand deathly quiet. The air is crisp but yellow, like the putrid urine seeping through the denim of an impatient boy. He tugs on his father's tattered flannel.

Several people enter and exit the rail car. A towering, dewy-bronzed man hovers above her, sliding his palm down sultry alloy. In a poised manner, she withdraws her hand apace, vigilant to avoid touch. She raises her arm fastidiously.

"Boo," he says.

She stares blankly.

"Am I that scary?" he asks, lowering his head.

"No, I just didn't want to be touched."

He holds his neck like an egret, nips to tuck while attempting to unwrap a piece of peppermint and strawberry gum. He brings it up to his lips and slides it into his mouth. The fetid fruit and leaf tickle her palate and nose hairs. The silver wrapper falls to the floor, and he drags his foot on top of it. She peers down at the wrapper underneath his shoe.

"What?" he asks.

She swallows. "No, what?"

"Seriously, nothing," she says.

"Am I bothering you?"

"No, you are allowed to stand there," she says.

"So, where are you going?" he asks.

"I'm actually in the middle of something."

"What?" he asks.

"Thinking."

"Mhmm," he says, licking his lips.

"Sorry," she whispers, tucking her hair behind her ears.

"I said boo, but you're the ghost. Your fingers are fucking purple and gray," he says.

Lassitude and passive, she scoots her bottom two seats down. He rolls his eyes and pulls his cell phone out of his pant-leg pocket. She sits, her knees kissing on the stale plastic seat, tucking her over-washed, carob-syrup curls behind lilac-blushed monkey ears. A fatigued mother cups her screaming child as the pitch of her shrieks matches the screeching tracks. She surveys the other passengers. She descries beauty in every character; in bellows and cries, in ignorant cherry cheeks, in raw lungs, freckled shoulders, porcelain chests, blemished chins, roman arks, purple eyes, in absurdity, and splintered smiles, omitting herself. Her stomach moans, hungry for love and ease.

As the chair marks her base, she observes the waxy-still perching before a spotless, metal-etched hand mirror. While examining a medley of mirror faces and lonely control, the cold musk of her imagined reality odorizes the interior's zephyr, like improper meat. The woman she sees in her reflection is unrecognizable. Her face transmogrified. Her features swim, warped in severity. An unknown face frightens her.

When faced with a threat, the human mind can hyper-fixate or scatter, leading to depersonalization, and creating a state of "unreality." Through her desire for perfection, her self-image has become distorted. Every monstrous creature, every rodent, and every animal appears in her features. She saw critters at first, then hybrids that slowly shifted into eviscerated mammals.

She subsides skinny as a rail, her waist striped with rusted-amber silk. Through years of callus growth around her rib cage, she has polished her public mask. Each body is blind to her frame of mind, the aching invisible to others. Her morale is virtually infrared, plagued by the loss of control and fear of weakness.

She is a rainkeeper. Weeping is a weakness. Rainkeepers weep plastic cries of frightening hopelessness. On wet nights, she would dance in the rain, embodying a keeper of teardrops. She'd call to the clouds to cry for her. The tips of redwoods blended into the sky, telling her it was time to settle down. Her heart would throb, and her blood would grow thick. Each night, after the heat let up, barking dogs went mute and birds tucked their wings. She either amused or scared herself. She'd lie on her stomach, covering budding breasts and thighs with her arms. The walls caved in and shadows drew pictures. She met the eyes of her ceiling lights and turned into a rat, sucking fish from the buttons of her mattress. Through visions and fabricated milieus, emotions would arise. The fictional cloth would unfold as actuality became perceivable.

She didn't live in a fantastical world, though her internal anxieties and worries misled her into seeing what she was most afraid of. The unsettling images in her head replayed like a scratched tape; a broken record, day after day. The intensive repeat was a continuous companion. The strenuous, heavy lifting fatigued her, leading her to lose control over her emotions at dawn and dusk. As a result, when she felt the desire to wail but didn't want to appear weak, she ran. She dashed through the rain, through the streets, past buildings, and to the train. Over time, she began to rely on unhealthy methods, lacking proper coping mechanisms. Those instruments became second nature.

Her toes tingle as they press against ebony leather, grounded on rubber. Static vibrations and buzzing inside her ears transform into a language she understands. Words get louder and her vision clearer. She allows herself to return to "the real world." Minutes of her day has been swept away, along with the dirt at the edge of the tracks. People boarded and departed, the train passing blocks and stations without her consciousness. Her feet aren't sinking into the mud of golden California fields. Her palms are no longer cupping honey bees. Stinger arrows never punctured her dainty paws, for her gentle nature protected her.

Occasionally, she thinks of herself as an apiarist, for her gut is a hive, not a cocoon. Control is lost when apiarists attempt to gather their bees after release. The honey chemicals swam through brain tissue; she had joined a vicious game. She was taught to fight herself; her mind. "Boss it back." The chemicals nick her away from the present, torturing and burning her.

The wiring of her own brain burns her like fine-cut paper encasing tobacco. She observes the smoke singing from the throat of a seemingly astute man. She observes his breathing pattern. He meets her eyes and gives her a head bob, lifting his chin. He sits, with his legs astraddle, adjacent to the now humming mother. She covers the cloven mouth of her baby.

"The other night, dear, as I lay sleeping, I dreamed I held you in my arms. When I awoke, dear, I was mistaken, so I hung my head and I cried. You are my sunshine, my only sunshine. You make me happy when the skies are gray. You'll never know, dear, how much I love you…"

A paltry memory surfaced as the lullaby was sung. As a little girl, she'd shyly performed this song for her younger sister. Fortunately, her sister inherited nothing resembling her mental health toils or complexities. While it wasn't jealousy that she felt, she envied her ability to move through life with more freedom and a lightness she'd never get to experience. Her thirst for ideals and perfection surfaced at a young age. The subjects of her obsessions were connected to preexisting worries or needs. As she grew older, experiences, occurrences, desires, and inclinations contributed to the exasperation of discomfort. She often howled paint, tearing down the walls of time, searching for control. While her sister could smile at minor blooms, she frequently sought unknown accuracy, perfected her canvas, and cleaned the surface she viewed as dirty, because of her inability to find a sense of serenity.

An old woman mumbles succinctly, "Shhhhhhhh."

The soft request for silence disrupted her song as well as her train of thought. She picks at the whitened tips of keratin on her fingers. Were the others going too? She studies a man resembling a hairless Sphynx. His skin is peeling and his eyes are celeste, framed thinly by spotted brown glasses that match his monochrome suit. She glances down at his freshly trimmed, receding chin, and then back up at his eyes. He appears gloomy. It's as if the moon flew in and stole the pinks and reds from the sky. His soul drained of its warmth. Wrinkles unveil the polarity of a morning man and a dreamer.

She turns her head to the left. There stands a woman, too restless to crouch. Her hair is tangled high with a pen through her knot. The ink tells a story; the lines on her back. They are just scribbles, an unnoticed drawing, but she could see pictures and words of stunning urgency and grace. She presumed she was the type to weave wreaths of grass and stitch flower garlands to place over her soft neck. She was the type to have a damp, dark coffin, with a face to weep for. She was the type to have tulips, daisies, and a face painted gold. She will have a stone-stained, china-blue, with royal gouache, but hers will be stained red, not painted. Karma stones and sap-bug jewelry ring around her neck. She runs her fingers along her bare, protruding collarbone, and steadies her breathing. Sudden shivers of flaring affliction control her breath.

She shuts her eyes and clenches her little fists. When her lids lift, there sits the old woman. She looks into her glassy, sugar-chestnut eyes. She stares at her with squirrel eyes.

"Dear," she says.

"Is it love, dear?"

"Is what, love?" she asks.

"Is that the reason for your sorrow?"

"What sorrow?" she asks.

"You look as if you are attempting to shut the world out."

"I am grounding myself."

"Alright, honey," she says.

She lifts her cheeks slightly, into a half smile.

"Is love killing you?" she queries.

"No," she responds once again. "I am just dealing with a lot."

"Well, I have spent my whole life loving a man that I can never be with. He was a man of all seasons. The type of man you could drink in all seasons."

"What do you mean drink?" she asks.

"Like coffee."

"I see," she says.

"What happened? Why are you upset?"

"It's alright," she says, "It's too difficult to explain."

"You can have it warm in the winter and iced in the summer," she says, returning to her "story." "Bitter or sweet; it helps soothe the throat. Maybe you prefer tea? It's the same, though."

She remains silent. Unable to find a proper response, she nods. She deems the woman rather unaware, blind to the functioning/manner of creatures' brains. She assumes the woman is a character whose mental state and lifestyle revolve around external or surface-level instances. She lives an internal life, with a highly mature view of her mind's psychology. This leads her to experience difficulty when seeking happiness. She believes that ones who can't conceptualize a deeper understanding of the human experience are the "happy" people; those with emotions revolving not predominantly, but rather exclusively around an event such as acceptance, exterior success, rejection, or death.

She analyzes the old woman and takes a sip from a metal water bottle. When she opens her mouth, succeeding her swallowing, she can taste the smell of alcohol. The woman is sipping bourbon from a water bottle, but she holds off judgment. The woman had just shared her reason for the afternoon painkiller. Her insides are so bitter that she doesn't require a lemon or lime to chase the liquid. Nothing would be sweet enough.

She presses the hairs on her arm and swirls her fingers around her darkened freckles and rose blotches like she and her friends did when they were younger. She is tired of being a soldier. She needs an escape. She is a self-crucifier, waiting for a rainbow to appear, waiting for wings to help her drift away. Never comfortable, she imagines ripping her skin and organs to shreds. When she senses the rise of consternation in her body, she regularly sips a cold beverage to reduce panic. She reaches her hand into her bag and pulls out a dewy glass kombucha bottle. She holds alcohol of her own, but much milder than that of the lady. She twists the rigid plastic cap and bubbles hiss. She sips the carbonated tea like a baby bird. The bacteria ease her tense gut. On an empty stomach, it swims faster.

She trails her eyes from seat to seat, catching the eyes of androgynous children dressed in powder pastels, a girl with red space buns and freckles, a lad with pods taped to his ear using masking tape, and a woman chopping carrots and beets on a cutting board. She attempts to imagine a perfect world, with perfect people and perfect circumstances.

By pondering her world in contrast to others, she feels insane. She routinely distracts herself while trying to trust that the subjects of her worries are acceptable or ratified, by controlling perceptions in her mind. To her, nothing is satisfactory. Her only wish is to go back in time and "fix things;" fix the unfixable or untrue. When she reflects on her past, she habitually attempts to alter, accept, or undo what has been done. Her heart is restless and stubborn. Letting go is Herculean.

Rationalizing reality is feasible in the lion's share of circumstances. She can certainly manage her sanity, but she often sleeps in her skull, unfurling imaginary situations. Her reverie draws her in with daylight nightmares and misleading, maladaptive daydreams. She may get lost, but her kindness and her care for the world (despite occasional hurtful barks of compulsion), bring her back to the subway. After all, every individual is essentially a brain and heart encapsulated in flesh.

Her skin swells as the blood bathing her bones boils and freezes. Perturbation dominates her hypothalamus. Her gut convulses as her thoughts knife at her insides, dizzy from conceptualized bleeding. Her heart beats fast, loud like a hammer. She can feel it climbing up to her face like an enlarging crack. She can feel it in her head like the failed sting-pecking that was supposed to lessen the pain. It didn't lessen the pain. It didn't lessen the pain. She cradles her empty stomach in her arms and inhales.

She reaches into her bag and pulls out an orange bottle, preparing for a potential panic attack. Triggers are scattered so widely that avoidance is almost pointless. She taps the opening lightly on her palm, allowing two pills to pop out. She places them on the back of her tongue, careful not to scrape the roof of her mouth or the back of her throat.

"What is that?" a little boy asks curiously.

"What is what?" his nanny questions.

"The thing she's eating," he shouts, stretching his arm out.

She answers, "That's not food, Tiger."

"What it is?"

"Don't point," she says.

"What it is?" he asks.

She scrunches her nose.

"Uahhh."

"Shhh, it's medication."

"Drugs?" he asks.

"Yes."

"Why is she eating drugs?" he whispers.

"I don't know, it's not our business," she whispers back.

"But I want to know."

"It's not important, Tiger."

"Is it bad?" he asks.

"No, the good kind," she exclaims.

"Drugs are good?"

She taps his back, "No, drugs are bad."

"Can I have some?"

"No," she says sternly.

"What if I ask her?"

"No."

"But..."

"No!"

The boy whines, and a woman next to him chuckles.

She couldn't alter the chemicals in her brain with concentrated doses of Sertraline, Abilify, Klonopin, or Luvox. She has always disliked the tickle of pills down her throat, but her skills rarely avail her. She was disintegrating from all of the medicine, but she wanted to rescue herself. It was just medicine, medicine she metabolized too quickly. Years of prescriptions could only dim the harshest of rays, but she was unable to obliterate the trouble. She could still be what she wanted to be, so she decided to try Transcranial Magnetic Stimulation. "Peck, peck, peck." She was just like a woodpecker; a perfectionist, with a fruit tooth.

Woodpeckers use their long tongues to slurp beetles, spiders, lizards, and fruits. Her tongue was tied; always restrained. She abhors the cage, but she wishes to remain hidden. She survives, hopeless, wearing golden-child armor and calling for an army.

Woodpecker

She raised a chick, a woodpecker, in a box. She fed its beseeching belly, surrendering to its bluff. Beaks repetitively pecked her brain. Her scalp stung, and increasing intervals startled her. She wasted time. The woodpeckers failed her, instigating a country bound flee.

A city girl bolted for the white country cottage. Damp stones tucked under blankets of grass paved the path to the doorway. The ice cotton had cried for another. Orange lilies enveloped the frame of the corroded cottage. Bees swarmed around the perishing plinth. She passed through the mint mud room to the living room; the room where Indigo-Tuscany fire dances in its cage. In the spring and young summers, new seeds are planted. Winters kill all that thrives, like the lies one's brain may speak. The lights were dead, the heat was shot, and the fridge melted the meat, but the warm glow from outside the cottage created vision.

Two honey-tinged floral chairs were positioned beneath two glass windows. Flowers increased in size from left to right and from top to bottom, like electronegativity arrangements. Through the grills, the pear-spotted lime hills were glowing, where the apple tree roots ran deep. The cottage appears eminently serene. It was her grandmother's hideaway prior to her estrangement, following her cult adjoining.

She climbed up a steep, bare wooden staircase. There were three bedrooms and one bathroom on the second floor. The wood beneath her feet was uneven. The walls shed where they met the floor. Each wall was dressed in a unique piece of paper. She had been here before, but it was better kept then. The house had been vacant for a while, and the upkeep has been rather sparse the past couple of years.

She wandered into the bathroom. Towels were cradled on a woven shelf. She twisted the faucet to rinse her hands, and the water ran cider. Behind her is a scale made of metal and glass. She stood before it, 5 feet 4 inches tall. She was not tall or scary, but she was strong. She paused for a moment before placing her feet just below the numbers, reading 97. She closed her eyes and ran her fingers through her hair. She glanced at the blue-stained bathtub. It's almost the color of chlorine.

She walked back through the doorless entryway and glided down the hall. After passing through the second bedroom, she came across another stairwell. The door had a minor cavity in the bottom. It appeared as though a rat had nibbled on it. She watched her feet as she carried herself up the stairs. The last step leads to a wooden board. She nudged it with her fists, before sliding it. Paintings of maples, willows, and rocks were sleeping against wooden chairs. The dusted desk had dried beaded pellets of paint. She clutched the painting and toted it back down to the ground floor.

An artist herself, she examined the landscape and textures. As she peered closer at one canvas, she spotted a poison dart frog. The brush strokes were fine, and the frog was small, hidden from the average eye. She is an eagle-eyed woman, effortlessly noticing ornate details.

As a child, she often viewed other children and familiar adults as various fruits, objects, or animals. She saw people as one of three fruits; an apple, an orange, or a banana, or one of four animals; a mouse, a rat, a bird, or a frog. Rats and mice are the most common, while frogs are among the rarest and sweetest (neglecting the poisonous breed).

She peered outside the window, directly across from the steps. As she glanced briefly, she caught sight of a pickup truck driving up the long gravel driveway. She placed the painting down against the bottom step. She met him outside as the car came to a halt. A rugged man with a scruffy beard opened his car door.

"Can I help you?" she asked.

"I don't think so." He trotted around to the cargo bed and flopped his arms around.

"Who are you?" she asked.

"I should ask you the same question."

"This was my grandmother's house," she answered.

"Ah."

"So who are you?"

"I am going hunting," he said.

"Hunting?"

"Yeah, ya ever heard of it?" he asked. He laughed and clutched a gun. He grabbed a burgundy backpack and started trudging up the steep, tall-weed hill.

She skipped after him, standing in the grass where daisies were once picked from their roots; stolen from the weak earth. The soul fires dried the soil and killed the fruits' babies, along with the owner of the wool that sucks her toes. The fields were no longer thriving, and they were alone on the hill, except for the anxious lamb belting song and burping baas from the moss-felted rocks, in the mouth of the rise.

"What are you hunting for?"

"Sheep, Deer, birds, wild goats," he said.

"Goats?"

"I don't like 'em," he said.

"Ok, I don't think hunting here is legal," she said, squinting her eyes.

"So what?"

"I don't know."

"I come up here once a month," he said.

"From where?"

"From the local sheep farm a few miles west."

"There aren't any hunting spots down that way?"

"There are, I just prefer this one," he said.

"For your information, this is private property," she said.

"You going to kick me off?"

"No."

"Ok then. What are you doing up here anyway?" he asked.

"Looking for some direction."

"Aren't we all?" he asked.

"Yeah, I guess, I'm just trying to start over or at least get a fresh

start."

"I see," he says.

"You see?"

"It's an expression."

She glared at him, "Yeah, I got that."

"Difficult aren't you?"

She stopped suddenly. "I'm going to head back down," she said.

"Alright," he mumbled.

She walked back towards the house and spotted a Kaka bird. It perched on a large tree in front of a stone fire pit. The Kaka is similar to a Kea or a parrot. As a child, she was compared to Kea in appearance. She was hardly a Kea, for she bore more resemblance to ravens; drawn to the comfort of what she knew, while essentially remaining ductile and curious. The disparage and affront were possible seeds in her current mental disposition.

Commentary, whether true or false, are all leeches that still suck rationality from her veins. The words and actions of others have been forgiven, but not forgotten. Her memory is too sharp for her benefit. She has slept along with winter, awaiting the green. Her skin is massaged each evening with velvet sheets. The velvet was tough, textured like the "outside" furniture beside the fire pit. Coats of water are drained from her pores while she dreams of cold comfort words, receiving whiffs of putrid cologne; one that paints a face that burns her eyes; an image that paralyzes her bones in the night, only to awaken sore and unrested.

A rotting barn stood behind the arms of a rotting tree. Small patches of sour green moss clung to the roof. She reached the door and noticed a large-ringed steel chain around the door handle. She yanked on the chain, and it fell to the ground, barely missing her toes. She entered the barn and squeezed past a 1980s moped. Dead leaves caked the floor. Rusted horseshoes were hung on bent nails. As she wandered farther inside, she stumbled across a leather trunk, rotting beside petal lamps. The opening was sealed with wax, thin enough for her to pick off.

She began to scrape the wax off with her fingernails before grabbing a stick. She lifted the lid slowly, unveiling old photographs, letters, charms, and an assortment of bones. It was dull and dark inside, so she lugged the trunk outside onto the grass. She emptied the items into piles; one pile for photos and letters, another for objects, and another for garments. The wax on the outside of the trunk had seeped inside as well. Among the array of items, she finds the terms of agreement for a self-help and a behavior modification "community," along with several images of a subway station. She examined the writing and images, finding that these were from when she first joined the group. It's intriguing how both she and her grandmother were studying to become forms of therapists.

While her grandmother was a general therapist, she wanted to go into art and CBT therapy. They were both psychological and deeper than many. Her grandmother would tell her, "You are spiritually connected to me." The "cult" that her grandmother was involved in was psychotherapy, mass transformational doctrine. She was a follower, motivated by a belief in striving for personal growth and transformation. The practices were often rituals and intense, documented group sessions. The descriptions were slim. This type of "therapy" is insane, but vulnerable individuals can be prey due to the manipulation and control of an authoritative leader. She'd, under no circumstances, get involved in a religious or physically harmful coterie.

Among the photographs, she saw a stream. The same stream was located just on the other side of the barn. She must have been included in the "secret" society or the leader's most valued members, for one of the common gathering spots were in her backyard.

Her property was a decent venue for wilderness practices and liturgy. Individuals seeking personal manumission and liberation would swarm through the valley pit and climb out to wake and rise. The streams edged with tall grass and Asteraceae acted as moats protecting the "sacred" valley.

She dropped the items in her hands. She skipped over to the nearby stream; a river of shame. The sound of the water trickling down the stream was calm compared to the mental waves she surfs daily. Her brain was an ocean, and she drowned in that sea.

She removed her shoes and peeled her socks off of her feet. She placed her feet in the stream and waded through shallow water. As she treads further down, the rocks begin to feel like razors and teeth. Her toes and ankles were raw pink like a lamb's skin. She could bear it, though, for she was keeping her mouth shut, running away from the world. While running away, she had been caught by a bullseye. She wasn't afraid, for the horns were within. When her feet began to itch, she stepped back onto the grass. The dirt clung to her toes like iron to a magnet. She grabbed a few items from the pile and placed them into a canvas tote bag. She then shoved the rest of the items back into the trunk. She left it sitting there in the middle of the field and walked to the edge of the pebble-lined road. She walked up to the front door, her tote bag in one hand and her shoes in the other. When she reached the turnaround, she noticed that the truck had disappeared.

She must have spent hours rummaging through her grandmother's things. She walked back into the house and realized she forgot to shut the attic door. Dead ladybugs and beetles lined the edge of the nearest window sill. She opened up a nearby closet to get a broom. She flipped the light switch and a dead moth floated down from the bulb onto the flood. The moth reminded her of her grandmother in the way that she was drawn to the light and spent her evenings drunk on heliophilia.

Her grandmother was looking for a way out of her misery and grief due to loss. The silence and absence as a result of death were deafening. She, too, was looking for a transformation. She had been battling mental illness and forms of PTSD for quite some time. Unfortunately, medication and TMS hadn't helped. She is an expensive woman. She fingered the piece of paper with the address, and like a crane, she hung her head and neck forward as if she were ready to fly; fly away from her inner conflicts and stressors. Her fighting wasn't enough. She was at war with herself. She tried everything, but orange and blue gnawed at her brain.

At night, she would look at the stars. One by one, they would appear in the Welkin. Diamonds of the enemy whispered lies into open ears, like slaves of the azure. She was tired, but she isn't on a bed or in a medical box, she is on the subway.

She feasts her eyes on the old woman with aged lips and frosted hair. The one with the sad love story. The tips of her sage-green headscarf pet the pages of an Aves species encyclopedia. A rich-brown bird with a pale belly is painted on uncoated stock paper.

"Hawks have keen eyesight and an acute sense of hearing," she says.

"Your enclosure has no lock." You need something to keep you from falling when the darkness comes. Mhmm. When the darkness comes. Fears will fade if you look into the light. Try to keep moving."

"What are you talking about?" she asks.

"Just words of wisdom. Do you understand what I'm saying, though?"

"Yes."

"Good," she says.

"Mhmmm."

"Mhmmm."

The woman is bewildering yet wise. She looks around to see if anyone else has been listening to this woman's "words." No one else seems to notice or care.

Sometimes it's better to stop fighting obsessions and compulsions. Where is the separation of love, personality, wanting, and obsession?

She repeatedly glances at a wrinkled woman, eyeing a blue-green coat that is the opposite of her own outfit.

She dresses in a frequently washed rotation of six outfits. Peculiarly, she abhors the color orange. The black and orange skirt is worn by virtue of obsession. Midnight mauve, salamander, emerald green, and sangria-mahogany are her colors. She prefers black, like her daily painted mascara and liner. She never leaves without her ritualized hygienic routine. Her thin, soap-dried skin and her thinning, over-washed mane shed profusely. She moves with a shadow of repetitive hygiene and ritualized makeup applications, intrusive thoughts, self-disgust, fears of being photographed, distortion, undo/redo and need to tell compulsions, and a sense of derealization.

She needs everything to be "just right." The pain is manageable, but it is unbearable. When things aren't the way she needs them to be, it causes her OCD to expand and increases the number of obsessions and compulsions. She knows that strength is paradoxical, and she must learn to be ok with losing control. She fears uncertainty and occurrences that have "ruined her life." She is tough. Like her grandfather, Professor, and Author James P. Carse once said, "Strength is paradoxical. I am not strong because I can force others to do what I wish as a result of my play with them, but because I can allow them to do what they wish in the course of my play with them."

She is getting there, but for now; she curls at the thought of her photograph being taken. She is haunted by past and future images. She avoids and deletes them, mitigating the pain. Her avoidance of triggers has grown more difficult, for her loved ones have become triggers in many instances. Breathless urgency for things to be fixed swallows her and freezes her sense of realism. Sporadically, the ice is broken by a stretched claw of rationality.

The train comes to another stop, and several new passengers step inside. One of which was a little girl. She looked awfully similar to her seven-year-old self. Little ringlets lined her temples, crowning the rest of her long, curly strands. Her cheeks were blushed, and tiny sprinkles mushroomed on her nose. She smiled, revealing two missing teeth; one incisor on the top, and a canine. She tongued the tiny white bump engorged in her swollen bottom gum. She giggled at nothing, able to amuse herself. She waves at the little girl, and she sways her hips.

"Hi," she says, with her fingers twisting the bottom of her shirt.

"Hi."

"What's your name?" she asks.

She opens her mouth to speak, and the little girl's mother grabs her by her shoulders and pulls her down to a seat beside her.

She travels back to when she was a little girl. When sensors are triggered within her brain, she can go back in time and recall sensory details, as well as recover her previous state of mind. It's exhausting, and she is crossing her fingers for the subway to take her where she needs to go.

Crane

She morphs into an alternate version of herself, viewing the world through an old lens. She was certainly a little girl, but naturally unlike the others. She was independent and quiet, unfortunately, aware of the darkness; the blackest gorges of visible mountains within this painful world. She was often seen as mature because of her lack of ignorance and innocence. She had always dreamed of being a beautiful woman. She was mannerly, gentle, and intelligent, but held her tongue. While she participated in the mindless activity of carving fairy dust out of buckeyes with her friends, her thoughts weren't as absent. Her thoughts were rooted deeper. While they loved stories and fanciful plays, she was drawn to the creations of homes and hideaways. She searched for "secret gardens," hidden messages, something to succor in her escape from the harshness she knew. While careless children left their playground projects to skip back to the classroom, she'd dreaded her anticipated strain.

Her perfectionism was disclosed fairly early; at the age of six. While children would scrape unsanitary boogers from their button noses or listen restlessly to their teachers, eager to learn, her thoughts were on a loop. She hyper-fixated on the sentences, the words, and the letters on her blue-lined paper. They weren't perfect enough. Her handwriting fixation interfered with her ability to finalize assignments; though she was a bright student, with remarkable grades.

She was an anxious but sweet child, unable to rid her mind of worries that a mother would disregard, or shrug off as "normal." When the stress of working became too heavy for her tiny shoulders, she sketched with pencil and color, in a book she was creating for her elementary school teacher. Her love of drawing was planted after discovering the control that picture-book tracing gave her. If she was able to draw over or free-handedly replicate the image she studied, she gained a sense of comfort and control. She wasn't fully deprived of joy. At least not at that age.

The stories, the games, the guides, the images, and the notions were all in the process of construction/design. They were young like her, staring at the glass of water beside her bed, watching as she woke with the yellow mist. The water inside her glass twirls and they creep in with the fog to heal, shield, and protect her; perching at the edge of her bed frame. The zephyr is dull and sticky as she rises from the sheets that must be washed. The sheets have been salted and sprayed by her body as she slept in a heated chamber; an oven that mirrors a ceramic kiln. She'd tell them how they must leave, how she dreamt of the endless white and cold tip pens. As they blethered and babbled, she said they were noisy and tiresome. They found her words to be fairly hostile. Some of them testified, some of them bickered, and some dried up. All of them wanted her to listen. They bickered over who was right. Like congealing blood, each hush begets a scream.

She fingers the vines running down her spine. She pokes the freckle above her right breast and drags her nail up her aching neck. She massages the tribulation lymph nodes underneath her wetted brown hair. They are rounded, like clammy stones tucked under blankets of grass and foliage; a genus of plants that grow near streams and rivers, similar to the brook at her grandmother's cottage.

She carried an immense amount of love for people, places, and feelings. She used to love the water; all forms. She'd wade her ankles into east-coast lakes, run through city water spouts, and on beach days, she'd search for butterfly-shaped seashells or wave-washed sand dollars. She'd prance along the water's edge, stepping on hidden stardust, as the water's stomach fizz cut the vast silence. She enjoyed the juvenile splash of seaweed waves, but now, in her rare swims, the seaweed chokes her, as she opens her eyes, letting the salty sea grow red chili legs around the whites of her eyes. Her skin is purple, with blue veins webbing around her bloody, red lips. Salt stings her chin. The water she thought of as "clean" was now dirty; the ocean was filled with fish urine, a whale waste sea, a human spit glass, the neighbor's pool, and a filth-drowned bathtub.

She was a stone that got washed away by the waves of her mind's ocean.

Water

Her thoughts are ripples of pain.

Tendril pouches are embedded

between ridges of her brain.

Skates; lying eggs sprinkle the pool

like black confetti.

The specks wash up

with the spit on the tip

of her tongue.

She isn't crystal clear,

gleaming, or glistening.

She is dense,

her eyelids struck

by purple lightning

that wallops the water's silver sheet.

The bones in her hand

are algae roots.

The thorns on her back

are rounded like the weak

waves of the ocean.

Her bruises are like splashes

of water on pebbles;

rocks lost within the spume.

Singing salt fights

the cold froth of desolation.

Leaf parts separate the flow of tides.

Winds grow and howl,

roughly pushing bodies

into a sophisticated sea.

Rising foam leads patient seaweed

swiftly to misty endurance.

Tangled beauty and honesty pull

dead seashells to the sand.

She was a kelp fly, swarming around a pile of rotten seaweed disintegrating into the sand. She was a black fly kissing the window, as her legs suck the sill. She'd watch the world through a warped, invisible barrier. The barrier was thicker and blurred in the event of change. She loved to travel, but her ability to feel comfortable and lucid was hindered. The fear acquired control over her body, freezing her in place, her wings melting in the sun's heat. She enjoyed nature until the promise of escape crumbled with the eroding coastline.

While she strived in many team sports and activities, the appeal of solitary fitness or pursuits, was greater. She preferred to rely on herself for control and success. She had the mind of an artist. She gravitated towards the words of a writer, the grace of a figure skater, the freedom of an equestrian, the adrenaline of a ball game, the stability of a surfer, and the power of voice. She was rather independent at a young age, determined, strong, and confident in her values and beliefs. She could leave home without sickness and build shelters to protect her clay fragility. She felt a similar volume of safety as she did in her own home, lacking a sense of security. Her family lit her home, but the light only scared her. She couldn't hide in the vulnerability of light. She remembered her dirt and sand sculptures, creating horses, mermaids, trees, and people out of organic matter and material. She'd dance with sticks, cones, and pebbles; placing heat-painted stones in a circle around her body, a shield once taught to her.

She was fond of the comfort of routine and familiarity, appending the repetition of afternoon consorts and weekly sleepovers, with her childhood best friend. She hoped that for her friend, self-crucifixion and lunacy were foreign. She could see how her contemporaries had been spared of their fret and rumination.

She wished to be healthy and rid herself of the colossal burden inside. She purported a life without her intricate entanglement and was frightened; frightened of losing her refulgence and acumen. She had to fight the notion that the Mephistopheles within her skull was her friend. It was as if the moon had chased the clouds away, waiting to see the color of her eyes; the color of her "scared" eyes.

As she celebrated modulation, the water she drank daily began to run milky, like a foggy sky. In the liquid, dead branches floated like bodies that had risen to the surface. She wanted to retrace the steps she had taken. She yearned to view herself as wanted when looking into a broken mirror. It was as if she was standing on a broken telephone wire with webbed feet. Patiently, she waited to feel relief and satisfaction. It didn't come.

She allows herself to stay in an unspoken serenity, watching time crawl to a halt. Her eyes focus on a pink speck of dust in the center of the room. The voices around her appear muffled, tickling her ears. The shoes strapped to individuals' feet zoom in and out of focus. Each pair duplicates. Reality and dreams blend in an unfamiliar landscape. She is unable to bring herself fully into the current timetable.

She travels back again. This time, she is stretched out across cracked, red brick. Rotting moss and Molinia Caerulea spout from the fissure. Her callow hair sprawls, covering a contiguous blood drain. A curly hose spits, the glossy pool a reflection of the mossy, cool pillow. She lets her chest bubble with panic, and the tools of trade effortlessly roll from tongue to lips. Her riverbed is dry; moisture is stolen by shame and guilt.

Like a summer day in disguise, a heat weasel eats her up. The sting was either condign or unreasonable, but she kept her composure. Knowing what worries were befitting, puzzled her. Fishy feelings wiggle through her intestines, nibbling at her seaweed veins like cheesy chips.

"Crack, Crunch, Crunch."

She follows the sonance of a cracker. Salt. Salt. Butter. She thinks back to a time when she was clean and fresh. The gold running on fingers turns to mold. She recalls the car ride home that coughed obsession like sodium cubes; a heavy chloride aftertaste. Her adorable sister rested her head on mink-fossil pants. Her hands were beside her ears. She had just gobbled a handful of cheddar goldfish. She licked the tips of her thumbs before sealing an empty Ziploc bag. The grease and cheese of her goldfish-kissed fingers left an invisible stain on her legs.

"Get off of me," she said, pushing her sister off of her lap.

"What?" her sister asked, her eyebrows pinched.

"You got your food hands all over me. Now my pants are all dirty."

"It's fine, I licked them," her sister said.

"That's disgusting."

"What?"

"You ruined my clothes," she said.

"No."

"Uahhhh," she moaned, with displeasure. "I have to change, and now I have to sit here with the disgustingness on my pants." She began to panic as her sister apologized.

This was when her food and body contamination flared. Weeks later, she crumbled as a cream lunch sauce dripped onto her jean-patched knee. She scurried to the restroom. She scrubbed the circular blob with soap and water. She choked paper towels in her palm, and she rubbed the paper to shreds against the denim. She spent the entirety of the day out obsessing over her need to change her clothing. After arriving home, she immediately tossed her pants into her laundry basket and bathed her bones until the water turned cold.

Slowly, she developed a variety of contamination-concentrated compulsions that weren't centered around germs or illness per se, but immersed in the idea of being "disgusting." She began to wash her hands repeatedly. The backs of her hands were dry, and her knuckles were scaly. Her wrists were reddened by soap suffocation. The duration of her scrubs lengthened along with the frequency. After months of unknown and confusing distress, she was diagnosed with anxiety and OCD at the age of eleven. She worked with a therapist who used a punishment and reward system, but nothing was worth the relief of compulsion, completion, and ease. She used tickets for money as a prize for exposure competitions. She was forced to perch on a leather countertop chair, with a singular gummy bear placed onto her pants or skirt. She would remain still, with the candy on her leg, for one minute, and then she was refused permission to change her clothing or shower. If she managed to sit with the anxiety of her clothing being touched by food until her regular bedtime, she would receive a ticket. Some of the exposures were successful, but she continued to develop more obsessions and compulsions.

Occasionally, she felt as though she were living in a silent movie. The words were stolen from her tongue. The producers (the silencers) came from the basement of her own home. She dressed in her own sin, holding her breath until she knew the truth. Colors faded into a desaturated film. Grainy spots would swarm in front of her eyes. She wanted to breathe again. The mundane, soft whistles of the wind, the loud shouting of neighbors, the pleasant purrs of a cat, musical chirps of robins and blackbirds, the unpleasant screeches of children, and the perennial hum of ceiling lights were drowned out by displeasing thoughts. She felt herself falling from the hammock of her dreams. Every desire, every positive is negated by her past and what she cannot do. The past refuses to let her relax. The memories are too thick to strain. She was too aware, too hurt, too regal, too tenacious.

A wrinkled map of skin; her cupped palms, form around powdered pills. She gags before her wrist reaches her neck. She closes her eyes and places the vanilla-coated almonds onto her raw tongue. Water pushes them down her gum-colored throat like river minnows. On wooden tables and sea-foam benches, crows begin to crawl shirtless, straining to purify, to re-cleanse. Little girls tissued underpants, but now she'd rather have the figure of a little girl. She was a princess who thought the queen was everything, but now her older chest reveals itself in murky-water bathing.

She would dip her toes into algae pools as the sun would set and watch the sky darken. In the swelled darkness, numbing heat infects limbs that disappear into an isolated basin; a gully where bruised, black-lavender hearts stain the ringed silt of a heavenly velvet like boundless beauty; beauty seen only when religiously kneeling for unnamed love, through naked discomfort. Flower girls genuflect, clenching thorns and aching for the lavender queen.

Muted mauve is raw, unpolished, and cold, like the ashes that cake her bones. She recalled the days she dreamed of womanhood. Sorrow was sown into her membranes. She felt as though she were an ugly, scrawny girl, and every picture she had ever taken screamed "repulsive" to her. Over time, pictures of herself grew increasingly distorted. Her appearance invoked tears and nausea. Her only need was that she was always clean, pale, and thin. Never hideous, never a monster, never dirty, never disgusting.

She wanted to be seen as beautiful. Beautiful and worthy; worthy of

something. She wrote a poetic excerpt about Flower girls. Flower girls; an

allusion to "Lavender's Blue;" a song from a vintage lullaby collection.

This hardcover book was one that lived in her memories. While she didn't

fancy reading, she loved writing and listening to stories. As a child, she was

read Uno's garden, Imogene's antlers, Stellaluna, Harold and the purple

crayon, Corduroy, Madeline, Pippi long stocking, Heidi, and when she got

older, The secret garden, The Little Princess, Little women, A mango shaped

space, Out, and The Girl With The Dragon Tattoo. She grew to love poetry

and psychological/ horror movies. She preferred watching to reading. She

loved a variety of films, Heathers, Gone Girl, The Shining, Gone with the

wind, Endless love, Girl Interrupted, Ratched, Friends, That 70s show, You,

Gypsy, Criminal Minds, Orange Is The New Black, Ingrid Goes West,

Skins, Fresh, Ladybird, Crush, Fear, Empire Records, National Velvet, X-

Files, Normal People, High Fidelity, Skam Espana, Edward Scissor Hands,

Orphan, Rebecca, and many more. She particularly enjoyed stories of

people that she felt were unique or interesting. While she appreciated originality, she also observed the characters and creatures that she found to be beautiful and loved. She wanted that for herself. She loved films, but now they remind her of pictures; pictures of others, and pictures of herself. The images are too anxiety-inducing and distressing. She would do anything to go back and never take a single picture. Now she deletes, refuses, and avoids.

White-Surrender

Her elastic skin will not wrinkle

from smiles, from laughs, or anger.

She does not feel anger, she feels pain,

upset by the distressing weeds of the world.

Her brow furrows, her lips curl, and her eyes squint.

She is silent when she's uncomfortable.

She doesn't crush glasses, punch walls,

or even raise her voice.

She remains silent. She avoids.

They say she has surrendered.

Her body is plaster; white shoulders,

white breast hills, white bones, and white legs.

She appears as though she is lying in surrender.

Not surrender of her strength,

not composure, but restraint.

Reptiles, beetles, moths, and pincushion moss

swamp her land body.

She has a body of a shearwater, and the prints of

others are a uniform sooty brown, dusting her

white throat, her white neck, her white chin, and her white lips.

Her thirst dries the sea-foam lichen

and crumbles mermaid scale sweet-gum.

Eternal weariness and tension keep her body wound

tight, resting low like a Cygnus columbianus,

less visible to those around her.

She is a quiet observer, an introvert, and a listener

protected by the shrubs encircling her surrendering body.

She had always loved culture, art, museums, film, music,

apartments, taxis, bricks, parks, plants, flowers, soil, sand, water; adventure;

nature. Though she was never spontaneous, she thought of herself to be a

nature girl. She was one with the rocks, the moss, the sea, the butterflies, the

bees, the sky. She was drawn to vein-branch trees, daisies, strawberry

picnics, berry picking, creeks, honey bees, koi fish, brick ivy, lake foliage,

butterflies, the clouds, the moon, cacti, fields, golden hills, crystals,

clementines, fire, oyster-beaches, collecting lipstick cigarettes, sculpting

with seaweed and sticks, horseback riding, ice skating, ball games, running, dancing in the rain, and tracing stars. Now she likes witch-like fashion, indie-vintage jewelry, skirts, jeans, vintage couches, cafes, stone angel sculptures, galleries, wine bottle candles, leather, floral drapes, stained-glass lamps, dried roses, postcards, traveling, drawing, and writing.

Her room is a collage of vintage purple-black red jewelry boxes, red velvet roses, coconut and flower sprays or deodorant, a brown flower mug, sketchbooks, poetry collections, psychological thriller novels, tide pods, dryer sheets and balls, flowers, kombucha bottles, makeup, sunscreen, ivy, a succulent boob planter, a cactus planter in the shape of a bird, sterling silver and stone rings, earbuds, leather gloves, a tinted glass jar, medication, a camera, a NYC train poster, a film photograph of nude women, posters, New Yorker magazines, vintage postcards, records, witch aesthetic decor and outfits, indie lights, vintage furniture, rainbow bandanas, an embossed leather notebook, jackets, skirts, dresses, shirts, tanks, jeans, shorts, Doc Martens, running shoes, a guitar, sweaters, a tapestry, glass and metal figurines, a tote bag-canvas-artsy, a lamp, a rug, an art nouveau calendar, a wallet-red leather, a passport, a claw clip, a Halloween movie DVD, suitcases, coffee, and a full-body mirror.

Finch

The train reaches the next contiguous station. It smells colder, but the busy shoulder-to-shoulder, limb-to-limb stickiness, was hot. It's hot, like the baking of her frame in a ceramic kiln. The scorch of the humidity melts the ink from her eyes. The sweltering constriction of her own design cracks her. Wetted brown hair flies like ashes from a pit. A pit like the flaming ball inside of her boiling stomach.

She searches for a subway clock. She doesn't find one, so she glances at her cell phone tilted upward in her pocket. It's 4 o'clock.

4 o'clock; tik tik too late. She couldn't keep herself grounded from floating away like a loose balloon. She told herself her hike was just a dream. "Stay strong." "Move on." Her thoughts were too loud, so she went for a fall walk. Her sedentary seating was interrupted.

Dirt-Dress Me Up/Dress Me Down

She was

Tonguing sand,

clay, and silt.

Burnt sugar coats her lips.

Butter yellow

and onion grass reflections

glaze her wide eyes.

Charcoal flowers turn to ash

as smoke pools grill golden faces.

Disregarded croaks bleed from her throat.

Bones shatter like fractured glass.

No funeral singers could rescue her,

to shatter bulbs, or turn the lights out.

Teeth gnaw at her; a tangerine peeling.

She knew it wasn't candy.

This wasn't a playground.

She pictured pastel walls;

an epilogue with fragile tears,

while afraid, simply surviving.

His hands are a brutal stainache.

Play pretend, sleep on the floor,

and trace cold shoulder constellations.

He is a deep-sea diver,

his Listerine gargling under her skin.

Just one look, it's a broken joke.

A troubled mind is nothing new.

Overkill howls, but she'll tolerate it,

for fall is just a season.

Clouds, candles, youth;

she can't handle change, looking for carbon

copies of new skin and familiar colors.

She's a soldier sinking, sick of it.

Wings break her back.

They wear her out.

She's now a girl on the run

from wrong places and shadow preachers.

She can't breathe safe and sound,

but her tears will dry on their own.

She rose from the ground, floating through feathered woods. Her voice failed her, but oak arms carried her home, finding her a place to rest her head. She swallowed the soot. She dragged her swollen limbs into the shower and drowned herself in soap. She thumbed the prints of "innocent" mickey-mouse, platy kisses. She scrubbed her skin raw, tugging at her tissue, scratching her cheeks.

She believed she was the ugliest creature to walk, to run, to dance, to gallop, and to prance. She didn't want to struggle in the Prussian shadows of the sea. She was drowning in a sea of lemon-lapis puffer fish and clotted currant blood. Her tears seep through her pores, but her cries are silent. Her lungs expanded, the salt choking her, as she tried to breathe. Her heavy lids cover her eyes like curtains at the end of a show, and all she can see is dirt. She sits in rooms that house both safety and pain. Between the flashes of a face and stomach twitches, she told herself that maybe one person thought she wasn't ugly.

From OCD's view:

"She can hear our voices whisper in her ear when she tries to wash her hands. Memories she must scrub off, crumbs to erase. She was hurt by everyone. All she wanted was someone to trust, someone to think she was beautiful. She hiked on and fixated on perfection. She turned her blood to paint and created pretty pictures to bury the throb.

"Dirt," we shout, surrounding her. "Can't you see the dirt?"

She kept the raw shame to herself, tossing clothing, and smiling for her caretaker, after returning home. She did what she was supposed to. She had seen him before, though she couldn't form a name. She chose to let him go. She suppressed it all, and not a soul suspected a thing. She didn't want pity. She didn't want to acknowledge the matter. It wasn't anger nor hate that she felt, but ache and torture.

We watched as she grew fond of the dark, a place she didn't have to close her eyes in order to pretend that anything could be lurking in the shadows; a monster or an angel. She prefers the shade over bright white. We can detect pure evil in crisp blankness. In the dark, it looks so pretty. The solidness of nothingness. In the track black, the ugly, the curves, the disgustingness, the dirt, the burnt, the shame, the guilt, the hatred, the pressure, the destruction, it's all hidden. It is enshrouded by the invisible, but not gone. She thought she had to cut the fuse and separate herself from us. She doesn't see it that way anymore. She still loves us. The deep delphinium; the image she begged for, has been destroyed.

She looks into the mirror, and we know what she sees. It's like Halloween in the spring. A plum face with a rose water spritz resembles beads of nose sweat. Her features swim like fish and pond ducks in a lake. Her nose burns with a perfume of raw meat and iron-infused bodily fluids. We follow her to the shower. She can hear our voices whispering in her ear when she tries to wash her body. Memories she must scrub off, dirt to drown, skin to erase. We told her what must occur, what must happen, what must be. We voiced our concerns, aiding her in the saving of her ruined life. She is disgusting; she is ugly. She must fix things. Her mouth is dry from dehydration. Every drop evaporates as her yearn for repose steals the liquid from her rind, like squeezing orange juice from a clementine. She is thirsty for satisfaction and relief. She can get that relief by obeying us, by listening, but her father tells us we are the juicer; that we need to go. She is fragile and sensitive, but not weak. If she gets rid of us, if she silences her voices, she will regret it. She will make mistakes. It would be to her benefit that she forces herself to hold on to us. We aren't trying to hurt her. We are trying to protect her. We need to stay. We only know what to do if she surrenders. We don't know where to go if she tells us to go."

She is a quilt; each rectangle a moment, a person, a trait. The stitching is firm and tight. A patchwork of ruin drapes over her as she tries to sleep. She rids herself of the comforter, changing her bed, but it comes back with a different face, in a different material, in a different shade. The stitching is slightly different, but her heart is still caught in the middle. She likes the covering over her body at night, but the tight fabric clinging to her body brings her only the coldest of comfort.

The texture of her current bed feels like a ripped, worn rug. The fabric was red and coarse on her skin, like the dulled burgundy mats she had seen at the cottage she had visited. She had been hoping it would bring her clarity.

Every warm spray of water, every ray of sun, every coat, every blanket; they only worsen the cooling of her body. Sleeping, curling on rugs, felt like lying on a stubble. She liked stubbles. She likes the rough clean cut, clean shave, clean control.

Rug

A rug is adequate for sweeping

bygone skeletons, ripped

magazines, dust, filth,

feelings, memories, and needs.

Occasionally, the rug is helpful

for hiding and concealing

what should be or is

sought to be hidden.

I am bedeviled by thoughts.

My mind slips into the abyss.

I'd get swept under the rug,

feet crushing my cranium.

The rug can burn,

leaving skin red and raw

while collecting dirt

from its crossers.

Its stitches are one

with my heart.

It absorbs my footprints

of fear and of confession.

Intermittently, people dig

under rugs, searching

for the lost in

infinite emptiness.

Sometimes, I sweep myself

under the rug, knowing

I'll be safe, appreciating

the shield and assurance.

At times, I think

I am the rug, letting people

walk all over me, letting

them stomp on my stitches.

Some rugs are torn

and scuffed,

some are dull and rough.

Some are soft and groomed.

Some are old and complex.

Some are stunning,

and some patient;

woven over time.

Some are

knotted with silk

and wool,

with pinks and blues.

Some are sewn with red

and dark ink.

Some are thin,

some thick.

Some are quiet,

some are loud, and

some have holes, bumps,

and cigarette burns.

I'm dirty, invisible, burned,

hidden, and tough. Who am I?

The swept one,

the burned one, or the rug?

Falcon

She aged, no longer a little girl, but she can still feel it. Her hymen is still sore. She can still feel something inside of her as she sits on the plastic seats.

At night, she curls into a fetal position, as liquid spills off of her head and shoulder, trickling down her stomach. The water tongues her toes. She shivers in 110-degree F licks. Her chest is Indian red, but her fingers are watermelon soaked with heather. She bathes twice, maybe thrice daily, still trying to clean her dirty body. She hid her suffocation when she began her high school studies at a school for the arts.

She kept her guard up when forming relationships. As months passed, she felt a little more at peace. Compulsions were rare, but her obsessions were still pervasive. She put pressure on herself to be perfect in all aspects of her life. She still loved the way her clothing clung to her body, hiding her skin from the world. Her long hair was a cape. She had been

fighting herself and her own thoughts for so long that she grew tired. She

couldn't find joy. She lost joy long ago. Her body changed, her breasts grew

plumper, and she began to fit into the low-healthy weight class with a BMI

of 19 (which she only maintained for a couple of months). She thought that

this is what she wanted, to leave her distinctly underweight self behind. Was

she pretty yet?

After looking at herself in the mirror most days, she crumbled at the

sight of herself. She needed to go back. Back to her "accurate" self. A

skinny, quiet child, with a BMI below 17. After a couple of months, she

went back to her underweight self. She made sure she went back down to a

16.5-17, remaining skinny/very underweight for the rest of her life. She

needed to be skinny. She needed to go back in time and erase the bad. The

mistakes she made. Her OCD forced her to not exceed the dangerous 97

pounds. She looks in the mirror and knows she is too thin, but cries at the

thought of anything more. So she remains 97, but she avoids

documentation. Her focus had shifted from others and their needs to her obsessions and compulsions. She used to be a pushover; doing everything

for others, sitting with her discomfort. Her compulsions got stronger. Her

obsessions with every photograph; past, current, or future, is extremely

painful for her. Her obsessions are larger than the hideous creature she sees.

She needs people, the people she cares about, to view her accurately;

physically, mentally, artistically, and aesthetically. Everything she did was

strenuous. Her room, her clothing, her rings, her demeanor, her thoughts,

her hair, her makeup, her laundry, her bed, her skin, her art, her grades, her

voice, her kindness, her strength, everything had to be seen accurately,

exactly, perfectly.

Years had gone by, and she was still hurting. She lived with a blade

in her back, shocking her into states of panic. She was and is unable to

breathe, shivering, and losing vision, with a burning stomach and tears

spilling. The pain choked her. She used her skills to sit with anxiety and

resist the compulsions

1.   It doesn't matter

2.   So what?

3. Self sooth

4. The relief will only be temporary

5. If you can't stop yourself, postpone

6. It's just a ruse

7. OCD is lying to you

8. Don't dance with the thoughts

9. It takes shape of everything you love and care about

10. The more you give in, the more control you are giving it

11. Keep busy

12. Focus on sensory details

13. Recognize/identify triggers

14. Boss it back

15. Don't waste time trying to prevent the thoughts

16. Sit with anxiety

17. Resist compulsions

18. Redirect your attention

For depersonalization

1. You are real

2. Ground your feet

3. Drink water

4. Observe sensory details

5. Photograph and re-observe

6. Distract yourself

7. Complete a ritualized behavior

8. Talk to someone you know well

9. Breathe

She used to be able to separate herself from the OCD and think

about it in a complex way, but she couldn't lessen the anxiety. She was

smart and began to be able to understand and talk about the way her brain

works to her loved ones and through art. Her wisdom wasn't enough,

though. She patiently hoped things would get better. She changed her

medication, and her doctors said she would be happy again, get better again.

There was no better. She had been hurting forever. She lost hope, but she kept focusing on her career and academic success, using her artwork as an outlet and as a way to help others.

"My artwork considers my ongoing battle with Obsessive-Compulsive Disorder and my need to establish order in a world that feels chaotic. I strive to share my experience with OCD through the repetitive recreation of objects/experiences, which are the sources of my distress. I address a multitude of struggles: obsessions, compulsions, anxiety, and depersonalization/derealization that come with Obsessive-Compulsive Disorder. The pieces reflect my battle to achieve accuracy and my need for things to be "just right" in every aspect of my life and work. Through my work, I am trying to find the balance between the grotesque and the beautiful; the discomfort and the solace. While creating artwork, I am working through my discomfort. I create it as a therapeutic activity and for others to gain something from my craft. By illustrating/depicting my battles and inner dialect between order and chaos, I intend to normalize the war with mental health that many people struggle with.

Through the manipulation of clay and metal in multiples, I

incorporate another layer of obsession to my work. I often utilize sculpture to create literal representations of the subjects that my brain spotlights. I use 2D materials to exhibit the emotional and figurative aspects of my diagnosis. For example, I fabricate an experience for the viewer through sharing my intense anxiety around past or future photographs of myself, contamination fears, and accuracy fixations.

My recent pieces illustrate personal coping mechanisms triggered by exposure to thoughts or experiences which cause me discomfort. When faced with a threat, the human mind can become hyper-focused or scattered. This can lead to dissociation or depersonalization. This creates a state of "unreality" which is the subject of many of my digital and illustrative pieces. Even in this distressed state, I continue to work and create. When the timing is right, art can become an outlet for anxiety. Through this work, I hope to manage my struggles with creating a "just right world" and help the viewer to come to terms with their own desire for solace and need for perfection."

She accepted that she was never going to get rid of her OCD. It is a chemical imbalance in the brain. This caused her to think it was her friend.

She was misled. She fears the day when she will no longer care about an

object, idea, or an instance that she believes to be important. She believes

that the taming of OCD will only cause her to make further mistakes,

ruining her life more completely. She is miserable, but she fears the

alternative. On the rare occasions where OCD is weaker, she feels anxious

and uneasy, as if there is something "not right" or wrong. It is

depersonalization or OCD, and neither option is enjoyable. She has used art

all throughout her life as an outlet for her anxiety. Her art thesis is centered

on her Obsessive-Compulsive Disorder, which doesn't provide much room

for her to separate herself from that part of her life. It is difficult to escape

that aspect of her life already, so the work, while most likely a beneficial

exposure, can flare existing symptoms.

A few of the pieces she has created are:

Compulsion Completion is created out of ceramic toilet paper and text. It exhibits her mind and train of thought in a state of panic. The obsessive

manipulation and recreation of objects with clay incorporated an additional

element/layer of obsession into her work.

Stranger In The Mirror is a digital illustration of her experience with

OCD and anxiety, and how that creates a state of unreality, leading to

depersonalization and derealization. This is when she does not recognize the

woman she sees in the mirror and the events, things, or people around her

who don't feel real. The piece is in a dark antique frame with clay-slip

footprints leading up to it.

Feeding Fear is a series about her strength and disguise of panic attacks

and dissociation, through surreal anatomical, natural, and realistic imagery.

Out Of The Blue is a fiber and video installation mirroring her past body

and violation trauma through hand prints; a growing, overwhelming pile

that covers her up entirely throughout the duration of the video. A portion of

the hands disappear, showing how the overwhelming state can lessen, but

the pain and the experience doesn't disappear.

Animal is about her anxieties and obsessions around physical and mental growth, as well as the tethering to her past and triggering people.

Hideous Distortion is about her anxiety around and fixations on past and future photographs of herself. She wishes to delete all existing ones and refuses to take any in the future.

Burning is about the ache and burn of the games or the lies in relation to OCD.

Fingers is about the distortion she experiences when viewing herself and her body through plaster and silver rings.

Flower Girls is about her wants as a child and desire for being beautiful. It is also about the pain she has endured and the people who have hurt her. It is a reference to a song in one of her childhood books. (Lavender's blue)

Still Dirty is a mixed media piece using soap to create popsicles that represent what she must wash off of her body, a bathtub for the obsessive and compulsive washing rituals, and text to demonstrate the obsessive thought process of thinking she is still dirty after numerous showers.

OCD Brain is about the dialect between order and chaos. Obsessive-Compulsive Disorder creates chaos within the mind, which drives a need for order and the performance of compulsions. The lights turn on in a random

pattern, mirroring how the brain puts a spotlight on certain subjects. These

subjects tend to be things that others rarely focus on. Once one thing is

"fixed" (portrayed through creating a pattern with the lights), the mind finds

another problem to hyper-focus on and obsess over. A sculptural element of

the recreation of Transcranial Magnetic Stimulation coils was designed to

be placed on the backs of the lights to demonstrate the therapies that have

been tested.

She wanted to believe that she wasn't a failure; a broken girl. Her

grandmother, of matrilineal descent, invariably told her that she was

brilliant, a spiritually connected soul. She recalled the visits with her

grandmother before her estrangement. She felt as though their minds were

similar in complexity and vision. While her grandmother did not share her

artistic abilities, she understood her struggles and doubts. Her grandparents

on her father's side, however, did share a portion of artistic and passionate

qualities, but they have distinctly divergent minds. They were less aware, in the same way that her father and sister are. This allows them to live a lighter life. Their emotions and reactions, like the woman on the train and the majority of her father's side, were based on external circumstances and affairs. Some could argue that living an externally grounded life is better because their struggles and issues are rooted in the temporary or true. Some could argue that living an internal life is superior, for their world view varies and differs greatly from the average individual.

She has a deep love for others, and an interest in culture and the unique qualities of the world. She is fascinated by the art, people, land, food, mannerisms, of different countries and cities. She has traveled to many countries throughout her young life. She has visited Greece, Portugal, Turkey, Israel, Jordan, Columbia, Iceland, Spain, Mexico, Chile, Thailand, Vietnam, Cambodia, Cuba, Italy, and London. Her favorites were Italy and Thailand, but her heart will always be with New York City.

Throughout her many travels and trips, she has come to notice that her depersonalization and dissociation can heighten during flights or transition periods. Change allows for either a mental improvement or etrogression/backslide. Travel is not the only trigger, for she is currently

remaining in a general pool/location and is experiencing a significant level

of discomfort. She knows she must do this independently. She has to fight

his. Her eyeballs spin around, like a head on a totem pole. No one is

looking at her, except for a dejected young man. He cracks her a smile,

revealing the sharp tips of his opal teeth. She imitates his gesture.

"You have white stuff on your face," he croaks.

"I know."

"You do?"

"Yes," she says.

"Why?"

"Why what?" she asks.

"Why did you leave it there then?"

"Because it keeps my face clear," she responds.

"Maybe you should use something else," he says.

"This works," she says.

He tilts his head downward to his dimmed iphone screen. He

scratched the indentation of where his forehead meets the bridge of his

nose. "Do I stand a chance?" he asks?

"What do you mean?" she asks.

"Before I try a line."

"Trust me, you don't want to be with me," she says.

"What do you mean?"

"You'll change your mind in 10 minutes," she says.

"Let me guess you've been in too many relationships," he says.

"No, one."

"Really?" he asks. "You've kissed one person?"

"No, not just one person. And that's none of your business," she

responds.

"So the person you dated, did he ever stand a chance?"

"Mhmm, that's the sad part," she thinks to herself. She turns away.

"You are quiet," he says. She nods her head.

"You seem like the person who builds too high walls," he says.

"I'd say they are a reasonable height," she says.

"Why is that?"

"I'm not going to tell you."

"Alright. What are you listening to?" he asks.

"What do you mean?"

He points to the earbud nested in her ear.

"Oh. Nothing, actually."

"Oh ok. What music do you like?" he asks.

"Indie, Pop, Rock, Alt," she says.

"Ok."

He turns the woman leaning against a pole to his right. "Hey," he

says.

"Hi?" she says.

"So, do you have to fend off guys a lot?" he asks.

She rolled her eyes as she heard him ask her that question. He is

simply a desperate man.

"Love," says the tarrying old woman, sighing. The old but comely

woman seemed to have aged over the duration of the ride. She was practically a coffin-dodger, biding so silently that she'd almost forgotten about her. She studies her face like a lamina castle. The wrinkles and lines caress the corners of her leaf-like lips. She winnows the echoes of laughter and smiles, and the indications of frowns and pouts. She traces the remnant-curtains of expression and maturity beside her eyes. She unintentionally catches her gaze. Both of them maintain eye contact. Both of them are uncomfortable yet stubborn, or unfeigned and unstirred.

Oxygen-Hard To Breathe

In the sharpness of gaze,

the sting of dryness,

and the lack of condolence,

we seek laps of solace

and strokes of restful slumber.

Touch can weaken or

strengthen bodies

like change, progression,

and augmentation of

the motherland's fastness.

Metal punctures muscle.

Chords strangle trees.

Cement buries grass alive.

The sun lights the earth,

bleaches bodies warm, and disappears,

abandoning its children.

It gets dark waiting for the stars.

Even they disappear into blackness.

The world is a wicked bliss.

For some, it's entirely wicked.

The fresh forests of oxygen burn

into flames of blue fires

that leave charcoal logs.

They steal the breath from our lungs

before a beautiful phoenix rises from the ash;

the ash of the dead, crumbled petals.

The ashes are used as tea for the weak young.

Like wild berries, mushrooms,

or ripe slaughtered pigs,

half of it's raw, bitter, or poisonous.

When the taste of love and pain is bitter,

sore hearts and throats suck on drops of candy

like peppermints burning throats.

They remind us of the ones we desperately

want back and who we pray to forget.

Even the sugar fights us,

taunting our mouths with cavities.

Following the repair of rotting teeth and

rinsing out mouths,

we must pump weak lungs.

Thick fractures of misery weaken bones,

cracking them like walls of a well.

The well is poisoned

like the filthy, toxic lakes and seas.

Our porcelain, painted skeletons

bathe in a concentrated juice of chemicals;

a juice like acidic blood bled by citric fruits

as they are cut down like babies

hanging from the ceiling.

Tears are used for blade brushes, and blood for paint.

Jaws are clamped as fists of sweat freckles

tongue stale, marble skin,

sending frost thumbs of regret.

Colorless-lipped,

oblique shadows

point warm dirt

toward twitching fatty dreams.

Sterilized spiral windows

box organdy squirrels

and muzzle chloroformed roars.

Bare weasel bones kill choking

spotted ducks in an oily hailstorm

that coats cigarette thighbones

as it repels the water in an attempt

to rehabilitate our legs.

Gloved paws turn apple juice

into dark-spotted candle wax.

The tiny plastic cups that carry water

are a reflection of the tallow sky,

provoking limp language and gestures.

Sparrow

She has an amalgam of a regal, puzzled, anxious, composed, and distraught appearance; a so-called cruel look on her face, resembling a dog. She won't bark, though, for her impulses are kind. She is a gentle person, occasionally mistaken for being cold. The ice was merely a barrier between her and further pain. She remained sweet at heart but tough on the exterior. She is compassionate, warm-hearted, and loyal. She gradually revealed her emotions, which was a healthy mistake. When the lid was lifted, bottled emotions and pain sprayed onto those around her. Her wounds only bled sadness or hopelessness onto a few because of her calming, contemplative nature. It didn't spray rage or resentment because she wasn't aggressive. Through her own need for control and accuracy, she can irritate and anger a few individuals, especially those who have ODD tendencies. She is scrambling to clean up the mess caused by miscommunication and connection. She continued to move forward. She still reminisces and obsesses over the past, but her strength has prevailed. She didn't play the victim, but she had difficulties forgiving others for their mistakes (especially ones that have affected her). She should have allowed others to know all of her. She's exhausted, but then again, so are others. She was too. She needed to breathe. Perfection strangles.

She listens, cares, nurtures, is sensitively sympathetic, and is kind, but she pushes people away, and it affects them. She failed to express her feelings to them. She has become more vulnerable. When she cries, she still feels ashamed and weak, but she is attempting to reveal her intellectual sentiments and composite fervors.

Words, phrases, and memories reside in her mind like bullets. These wounds led to infection. She, however, is a fighter. She has soldiered on. "Strong, Strong, Strong, endure the pain until it passes." Is there something better?

Her phone buzzes, and she flips the screen to see her reflection after the notification fades. She abhors her reflection, but she ignores it. The alert reminded her to complete a survey, which included questions about the improvement or regression of her intrusive thoughts. She was transported back to the time between TMS sessions. She'd wander around the cacti gardens and gated statues. She admires one in particular; an angel with her head resting on her hanging forearm. This was the subsequent most exquisite angel sculpture she'd ever seen. She remembers hunching over the skirt of a copper-stained, stone fountain. Tossed pennies sunk to the bottom, forming a blue patina. The teal paints the clear water stale. She presses cotton balls against her scabs, like silver kisses of pearls, in oyster shells. Like SCOBY, her rotten leather has dried but was waxed tough. An angel floats in the center of the fountain. The undercut of her wings is gray and chalky. The smooth surface of the angel's cheeks are disintegrating like cut flowers, watered in the mouth of a sink. She strokes her finger, by her own embellished, berry-colored cuticles and bitten hangnails. The angel was quite delicate and peaceful, unlike Haserot's Angel. The statue is death's guardian, appearing to be weeping black tears that drip down her aging, bronze form. She is doubtlessly daunting, but indubitably beautiful.

A Statue

She stands,

still and hushed,

silently watching,

waiting for disintegration.

Hollow words of mockery

kiss elements of the ground;

elements that sculpt a slender figure.

Chiseled eyes appear shallow.

Perhaps they are deep,

stuffed with memories,

misery, wonder, and wisdom.

Frail glances awaken

statues; bodies of the fallen,

from an impotent rest,

or of dark and bloody wars.

The stone and metal

of death reap the forgotten.

We weather with patience.

Her hair is made of loneliness.

Her heart was written

in blood; blue blood turned red.

Oxygen and carbon kissed,

her limbs broke to fit a mold.

She let her needs,

her connections, and herself crumble.

Knives carved into her skin.

Her soft interior folds, but

her exterior is rough and stubborn.

She is often trapped in the past.

Her mind debars her from the present.

She is immobile, hunched over with grief,

wallowing, and whimpering.

She appears sad, but she is strong.

She is strong, with a heart of silver and gold.

She forgot about her heart.

She forgot about the love,

about her loves.

She failed to fight.

She shut them out.

She ceased to shower

them with what she lacked.

She should have prevented the ruin.

The figures and forms

mourn the loss.

They mourn the pushed away,

time taken for granted,

seconds wasted on fear and retention,

and minutes swallowed

by past fixations.

Now they are frozen;

frozen in their regret, in their mistakes;

frozen in the ache of youth

and the age of time.

She let her mind take over.

She was lost.

She failed to keep what she wanted.

She let it all go.

She secretly cried for the things and the ones that were gone. She

should have fought harder; she should have endured the pain for longer.

The posing of statues lures her into intense analysis, similar to her

intrigue about the beheaded Medusa. She was interested in the fear, pain,

desire, and power of statues, both stone/marble or metal. She could find

hints of her own vehemence within the carved, chiseled figures. She always

thought of herself as a ghost. Her body is delicate, her bones are fragile, and

her organs are made of glass, stone, and feathers. When she felt herself

falling, she felt that she was one with the leaves floating down, forming a

pile; an accumulation of her woes.

She requires four things; to not be hideous, to have always been thin

(slim/skinny), to have never been disgusting, and to not be too tan. She wants to be who she wants to be, and to be loved. She attempted to agree with others who told her what was true; that she was beautiful, always thin, never disgusting, had ivory skin, and that she wasn't worthless. She grew to be so fused with OCD that she genuinely doesn't see those things. She couldn't fight the lies. She didn't want to fight lies. When she needed proof, the words of reassurance, the truth, she couldn't get it. The one person that she needed it from, confirmed her beliefs by failing to give her a proper response. It is too late now. Nothing can change her mind. She sees herself as fat, hideous, and disgusting. It doesn't matter to her if she "gets better," for she'd only be dismissing what she should be focused on, what she should care about. She needs to make sure she doesn't ruin anything else. She will force herself to never lose what is helping her. She is stuck. She is wielding all of her strength within, to fight this. She is drained and fatigued.

One would assume that her OCD would have hindered her ability to be a bright student, to manage; to function. It hasn't, for her perfectionism has fostered her ability to maintain a high GPA, and to keep creating, to continue on her intended path of success. She is vying with her shadows.

She is migrating.

She looks over at the open book, caressed by fingers of stretched skin. A sparrow is nested on the page. She shelters her body. Her arms are twigs that rest across her breasts and slide between the crease of her anxious thighs. She'll only shed with time, her feathers and eggs. The sparrow is a diversion; a diversion like the mental dance with a purple clown or a vexed ghost. Obsessive trammel ensues productivity. Her OCD improved the quality and depth of her work. Her fears, her worries, her pain, it haunted her.

A ghost

I love my pale plastic flesh,

Lathered in sunscreen, weakened by salt,

I love my brittle bones,

I love the mascara-black tears that seep into my indigo veins.

I love the stranger in my mirror,

The unrecognizable reflection,

I love my distorted, warped world,

I love that I feel unreal.

I love the obsessions,

The compulsions that swallow me whole,

I love the pit growing in my gut,

I love my hands washed red,

The violet in my nails.

I love running from cameras,

Deleting my presence,

I love the haunting photographs,

The hyperfixations.

I love the pills tangled in my intestines,

I love the false exigency for dressing in my green t-shirt,

I love the constant search for just right,

I love the repetitive visuals.

I love my shaking knees,

My fast-beating heart,

My hidden discomfort,

I love craving accuracy,

But never reaching it.

I love the echoing dialect between order and chaos,

I love the acid in my uterus,

I love the bitter dust on my lips,

I love the fingers plugging bloodstreams.

I love the hardened cuticles scraping my arteries,

The thoughts nipping at my wrists,

I love showering in exposure,

The water licking my toes.

I love spiraling out like octopus tentacles,

The ink seeping through my pores,

I love the air too thick for my lungs,

The suffocating fear,

I love the blinding illusions.

I love the blizzard in my iris,

I love the silence dancing in my cold throat,

Except I don't.

They come back; the compulsions and obsessions come back. They always do. She had been able to fight the contamination compulsions once before, but her belief that she is disgusting has resurfaced. The subjects of consummation control one's life. She is the same as she has always been.

The green shirt. The same compulsion, a different green shirt. At the age of three, she would habitually wear a green t-shirt with light leaves. She was obsessed. Her brain was different, even then. Eventually, due to her age, she grew out of the "phase." The same compulsion came back, the same mindset. She will always be the same little girl, but much older now. Her mind is built of many layers, like a pine cone. Memories and thoughts; they all track like paw prints. The thistles of pine trees land on the binds of crouching backs. The sun turns the cones fire-roast golden, as the burning of her pale peel shimmers, to prove she is alive. Her chilled, overheating body is thirsty for ripples of water. Her mouth is dry from dehydration. Every drop evaporates as her yearn for repose steals the liquid from her rind, like squeezing orange juice from a clementine. She doesn't get twenty minutes without obsessing. She was shoved in a box, and she is trapped. No matter where she goes, school, home, New York City (her favorite place), it is internal, so it follows her. It follows her, knowing how easily it could wrap its hands around her waist. It thinks she is so fragile that her protruding pelvis will tear the skin. She is sensitive but not weak. She lets her hair fall off of her shoulders, never tying it, waiting to be free. Now she sits on a subway, traveling back in her mind, trying to fix the unfixable.

She glances back over at the old woman.

"Would you like a sip?" the woman asks.

"Oh, no, thanks," she says.

"You sure?"

"Yeah."

"Wine can loosen you up. You look tense," she says.

"That's ok. It's ok."

"Try to relax," The old woman suggests.

"That's impossible for me."

"It's all about mindset. Focus on something else."

"That's really not how it works," she mutters.

She could never understand the inner workings of her mind. Most people struggle, but they never quite understand another's situation. She supports her heavy head with her dainty wrist and palm. She wants to close her eyes, but like stars in the dark, you don't go blind. When her eyes are both open and closed, she can only hold the thunder. She has retired from her work as a rainkeeper, for she has begun to fail at containing the water. She has concealed too much.

Touch

Our veins derive

from one bloodline,

yet detrimental, critical remarks

spun like spit off of your

diabolical tongue.

I recall the malicious measures

taken in an attempt to destroy me.

You don't remember

the day in the cottage;

the afternoon on the couch;

the moment you

placed your putrid

skin on mine.

The breath from

my lungs pushed

to the shore of my mouth;

my quivering lips.

I was turned inside out like the

underwear on our heads as we jumped

on the bed the night before.

The underwear on my head;

the underwear you stretched

with your chubby hands.

The fabric dug into

the side of my thigh;

the cotton I tried to clean in a bath

that I was forced to take with you.

In the bathtub, you cut

the side of my foot,

leaving a scar white

like bones are supposed to be,

but my bones are deep indigo and blue.

They are blue like water

or the bottom of a pool.

We had a pool outside

of our tasteful house.

A pool outside a house;

a house, not a home.

It was a family pool

behind the back of a house.

You wanted to play house.

You wanted to play

the man, and I the wife.

You wanted my baby.

I refused, and you,

nearly a toddler,

forcefully pressed your

stomach against mine.

Now I don't want to be touched,

not because I dislike

the way skin against skin feels,

but because it brings me

shame and regret.

Every warm hand and every cold

finger that touches me hurts.

Between color and weight,

through black frames around

my tired eyes that will wash

away in the pool

outside the house,

I still see you,

still feel it.

Though your attempt

failed, unlike the next man's,

it was the first moment,

a moment before many to come,

that I felt utterly,

repulsively

disgusting.

I may have been a

tattle-tale about the little things,

but I never told.

I protected both of us;

both of our innocent characters,

but I cannot any longer,

for you may forget, but I relive it everyday.

I relive your touch,

the next touch, the worst touch,

the dripping red little girl.

I felt disgusting and ugly for years,

until the worst touch, from a stranger,

but to me, your touch and his molestation

hurt the same.

She is an intellectual, lacerated sprout. She is ascertaining her roots and planting new seeds. She is supraliminal of her withstanding character. She is reliable, kind, trustworthy, humble, hardworking, persevering, stubborn, gentle, quiet, observant, wise, passive, strong, stoic, and understanding. She oscillates between pragmatism and amplified reaction. Is that stereotypical feminine behavior? She, like many women or "feminine" people, is used, manipulated, treated poorly, disrespected, and seen as emotional and too sensitive. She wants to be respected and loved.

Her character and traits were visible in her sleep, constant, even when no one was watching. That is when individuals' true characters are revealed. She needed control and to feel free. She felt stuck and powerless, in a world where parents have the dominion.

During her adolescence, while she felt out of control within her limitations throughout daylight hours, she was marginally more in control at night. She had control over her practices, activity, and noise in her extant free time, as well as dreamt proceedings. She used to be a lucid dreamer. In the end, even with the little control she had, she always gave the bad guys what they wanted; both in her dreams and in reality. She stopped, and now she is a bitch? She deserves a fuck you?

It's not only the bad guys. There are unfortunate accidents, traumatic experiences, losses, and health issues; physical or mental. Some push through their hardships, some result in unhealthy behaviors or habits, some to cults, and some give up. She wonders how others have handled their "problems." She thinks back to the cottage and the trunk full of memorabilia. She contemplates the reason for each person's transformation, evolution, or convergence. She writes the story of each individual, her grandmother's past, and her own past.

In her dreams, she is unable to move, sinking into the mattress beneath her sheets. She is trapped in a room, with monsters looming behind her bed frame. She feels her teeth, her lips, her face, and her body rotting; decomposing. No amount of regret can change the past, no amount of medication can unravel the truth, swallowing erasers will not correct mistakes, fingering photographs will not make them disappear, slitting eyes won't hide the truth, cutting out one's tongue will not save one from the voice in their head. Pressure does not equal perfection. The pressure of expectation, self-worth, and success can turn you into a diamond, or push you beneath the surface, turning you into the bones within the dirt. Pressure punches her back and crushes her heart as she attempts to sleep. Night is either peaceful or torture.

Nightingale

Nightingale: nothing (The nightingale has been sent to an aviary, where it has found a new nightingale to mate with). Despite all the things that hurt her, she is tremendously apologetic for her contribution to the mess. She is aware of her mistakes. She thinks about them relentlessly.

Nightingales have an astonishingly rich repertoire. Connection, pleasure, and infatuation are complex. Love can be the source of darkness or the stars within it; It can be unfeigned or deceptive. Love speaks, commonly crying at night. Male nightingales, that sing nocturnally at dusk, are perceived to be single birds, intending to serenade migrating females down.

The nightingale is bemusing. Spinal shivers are induced by the pitch-perfect harmonies, perfectly delivered lies and beguiles, and the pretentious voice and song. They can be calming as still water, but they are as treacherous and dangerous as a devouring wave. A presence can bring ease or anguish, moving nubivagant through the atramental sky.

She was uncomfortable, as if she were impluvious (soaked), her skin was soaked with the blood of a mazarine landscape. The vapor of her breath is cold, and the taste of her spit is becoming more difficult to swallow. Her lips twitch, her eyes blur, her shoulder shivers, and her hips sink into the tight plastic beneath her. Her body is weakening, and her frame is easily moved by the train's motion. Her stomach hurts, her legs cramp, and her neck swells. Her tolerance is increasing and vacillating. Nothing is more excruciating than a lack of love or love itself. Her elegance, tenderness, perspicacity, gentility, and a colossal sense of care shall remain, but romantic love threatened to take them away from her. She had devoted a substantial amount of time to shaping a perfect relationship, essentially enabling engrossment. She covets to be wanted. Now she feels unwanted by the only people she ever felt wanted by. It scared her to know that one's perception of someone can be so different from who they truly are. She had fallen for someone through her own imaginary persona and situations. In reality, he didn't match who she thought he was. She gave him what she wanted, and in the end, she took the blame. She sits, she stands, she walks, she climbs with shame.

She needed to breathe in order to be free of entanglement, free of alluring song. She sought contentment. Her introduction to romance was not entirely negative; there were several positive aspects. She hoped those details would be remembered. She wanted to recall why their love grew. Through patient practice, she ceases capitalization of the negative. She returns to her exterior environment, shifting her focus onto the milieu.

Two feminine women enter the train with their arms linked. One head rests on the other. Two locks of dirty blonde hair mingle on one shoulder. The hair-covered shoulder is blanketed with a European, finely knitted, hickory-smoke sweater. Her blue, beaded necklace dangles from the loops around her chiseled collarbone. The other woman is clothed in a bright green dress with a pastel blue headscarf that compliments her lover's necklace. The sweetness and delicacy reminds her of herself, specifically as a young woman. She is gentle and intricate, but harsh and particularly critical regarding a past love. She can and will take responsibility for her own faults and her own mistakes. She is far from perfect and can admit it.

Despite it all, despite the pain he caused, she really, honestly, truly cared. She was misunderstood, for she did it all for him. She feels as though she has let her OCD and PTSD get in the way. Toxic or not, she never stops loving.

Condensed timeline of intense relationship:

-Dating-baffled that he somehow fancied her.

-He prompted her to vacillate her self-criticism and lack of self-love.

-She was detached and self-reliant. She preferred independence and refused to let anyone know her entirely. He was dependent, pushy, manipulating, possessive, impatient, asphyxiating.

-She felt deluged by pressure and the unfamiliar. She was continually anxious and distressed. Physical affection was irregular due to her dislike of physical contact/touch and her past sexual trauma. Her OCD contributed to issues and difficulties within the relationship. She participated in some physical contact forms of affection. She relied heavily on other forms of displaying affection.

-She wanted to be able to do certain things, but she just couldn't.

-He fell in love, or so he avered.

-She did briefly. The strength of her feelings was evanescent. They were like vapor amid her youth. They would have been perpetual if it weren't for the pain he imposed, her OCD, her PTSD, and her languishing mental health.

-She remained distant, but she attempted to make him as happy as possible. All she ever wanted to do was that. She pushed through her own discomfort. She tried, she compromised. She did things for him.

-He wreaked pain and left damage with his toxic behavior and disrespect towards her boundaries. She was emotionally drained, milked, and her body was twinging. She managed to hide her anxiety and pain from him.

-She thought that it was all an attempt to get closer, that maybe he cared, or maybe he could just love her well. That he would respect her.

-She ended things as it was deteriorating her mental health and she was losing feelings due to his actions, but she genuinely cared. He handled it badly.

-Her leaving in the name of her well-being was construed as abandonment.

-He continued to contact her, trying to convince her she was everything. She felt sorry for him. She wished things could have transpired differently.

-He besought her to stay.

-He found a rebound.

-She progressively got worse, and he grew to be an even bigger trigger for her PTSD and her internal stressors. She decided that she never wanted to speak to him again. She asked him to refrain from contacting her, and she did the same, for several months. Over time, her OCD got stronger.

-They began to talk again.

-She needed a favor and he complied.

-He said he was still in love, and wanted to spend his life with her.

-She tried to make it work. She attempted to give him more chances, she tried to forgive him, for she still cared, but she was incapable of starting fresh. She wished things were different, or the situation was more ideal. She needed everything to be "just right" in order for her to build upon the relationship.

-Due to past actions and events, he was a source of trigger. Her OCD flared and PTSD got worse. She was flip-flopping and became contradictory in her attraction toward him.

-She cut contact again after spending a substantial amount of time and energy on him. She needed space, it didn't mean it meant nothing.

-She found it difficult to forbear compulsions. When she spoke to him, she would have to go back on her words, or compulsively say that it wouldn't/ couldn't work, due to the triggers.

-It was her OCD taking over. She also thought maybe she needed to be free from it.

-She hurt him by saying it wouldn't work and by alluding to the fact that it didn't matter to her. She just didn't think she could do it forever.

-She repeatedly said that she wanted to leave and that talking was hurting her more, while he pleaded for her to try and stay. She told him she wanted to leave and that he should stop feeding her compulsions.

-She told him she would control herself and stop texting. She did it for a while.

-She dithered regarding leaving. She considered the continuation of her efforts in figuring out how to be comfortable and at ease in the relationship while making him happy. She gave it her all, and she finally figured out how to give him what he wanted, how to push through, how to endure it, and how to fight her OCD.

-She had been advised to wait, to take time to figure things out, and think things through. The pressure was so high, but her body had been drained of blood. Blood from her wounds, so she took a break from it all. It was a mistake, for she "lost her chance."

-He was mad and angry, and he said he is done and wants someone else.

-He hurt her in the end, proving her doubt. If it was that intense, then it wouldn't be too. late. She really didn't know him like she thought she did. She did everything she could. She wanted to be seen accurately. She wanted it to work.

-He was exhausted, furious, done.

-He could possibly still love her, but it's probably for the best.

-For her, it was all torturous. Maybe he'll regret it, maybe he will in the future, or maybe not at all. She granted him a non-retracted display or disclosure of care.

She implored him to let her go; to fly away; to allow or acquiesce her to waive and flee. Eventually, he did; presumably sated and disgruntled. She hoped it was by dint of deference and grace, rather than simply a lack of love. She can cognize that due to his disposition, if it was on account of anything other than a loss of love, it was exhaustion, enervation, or wrath. She inherently solicited his moving on; his conclusion, but it stings her, nonetheless. She allowed her pain and Obsessive-Compulsive Disorder to interfere with her ability to discern that he, a human, can evolve and change. In the end, he confirmed her intuition that his actions and his so-called "support" were always by virtue of his own needs and his own desires, his own issues, his own insecurities, his own ego. Though she may have been rightfully cautious, she consistently fails to grant others the opportunity to love her completely, to break down barriers.

The circumstantial matters that prompted her to initially call it quits as well as the ways in which he hurt her; his habits, manipulation, coercion, whatever they were, could have always been an effort to get closer. It may have been his immaturity or her obstacles. Maybe, just maybe, it was worth it. Maybe, just maybe, he meant what he said. Maybe, just maybe, she should have stayed. Maybe he let her go because of the pleading, the pulling, the OCD, the confusion, the exhaustion. Perhaps, it wasn't a lack of love. In this, she was merely a caged bird. She wanted the cage to remain open, allowing her to come and go as she pleased, but not for the cage to open and lock behind her.

Love, in her mind, is limitless. If it vanishes, like dust or feathers on brittle bones, it wasn't heavy enough to mean anything, powerful enough to count. She trusted and had faith in a manipulator. She sought out the positive and the possibility of growth in his eyes. His beautiful eyes were simply a mask to hide the pain he had inflicted and would continue to inflict. He proved her doubt to be anything but paranoia. On numerous occasions, he was smothering or purposefully spiteful. His feelings for her may have been greater than hers for him, claiming to have been madly in love, saying he'd want to spend his life with her (even after she terminated their relationship due to his hurtful actions), but she never stopped caring, never lost fidelity, and her soft spot never hardened.

Regardless of the fact that he "physically" existed as a trigger, the distressing memories, contradictory quandary, and complications, she persevered; endured the pain, conducive to his happiness. He contributed to the aggravation of her PTSD and OCD symptoms. She didn't realize her mind and heart hadn't forgotten. She was aching from their harrying past, but she couldn't stop caring. She couldn't forget. He assumed that walking away was easy for her, that in an instant she would wave a magic wand and erase everything. If that were veracious, then she wouldn't have spent considerable time and energy attempting to please him or trying to fix things during and subsequent to their communication.

Amidst the agony, she proceeded to vindicate him. She was dragged through hell, but cannot hate him. She wasn't perfect. She had nodi to resolve. Given his persistence, she supposed his adoration was pure. She forgave him for his pushing, manipulation, harm, and disrespect, but it only fueled her obsessions and compulsions. It was too torturous. It got the best of her.

She toiled to justify, repair, rectify, amend, to trust, making an exemplary effort to fix what she could control, and to accept the impossibility of everything being "just right." In contempt of his unhealthy, detrimental behavior and the fading of her feelings, she tried. While she pushed him away and left, severing ties and killing hope, she also did a lot for him. It wasn't intended to hurt him. Upon her second or third sever, she began to question herself. She aspired to be worthy of love, so she assumed that if he claimed to feel that deeply and begged her to stay, the love was genuine and unconditional. Yes, he made mistakes, but she intended forgiveness. Nobody is flawless. The OCD took over, independent of whether the relationship was healthy or unhealthy, positive or negative. She is fighting harder than ever to ensure this doesn't happen again.

She had always desired true love. She doesn't believe in soul mates, but she dreamed of a love story in which she and the other person have only been in love with each other. A love completely and obviously more meaningful than the previous or the ones that could follow. She wanted a fighter; someone who would remain at her side, despite her complexities and need for periodic space or independence. She wondered if she was almost there. In the end, she was there for him when he needed her, and despite his intensely obsessive character, he wasn't there for her, unless there was something in it for him. It wasn't his demeanor to be kind for the sake of being nice. It took her far too long to recognize her steep expectations. When she agreed to give him another chance, she discovered that the conversation was too triggering. It foisted additional pain on her. She needed to leave once more. She repeatedly asked him to leave; to let her go, for she couldn't forbear her consuming compulsions. He finally pulled away. Was that what she favored? What did she need? She hollowed out hope, not because she didn't care, but because it was too much. It was too intense. She chooses and aches to believe that it was worth it, that the feelings were real, that he was only gone because of what she had ruined, that irrespective of if the outcome is ideal or right, that it will always be as great as it was thought to be. She gave it her all; she knelt for him. She hoped he was an angel, someone to provide her relief, happiness, or comfort. The wings were fake, they were stolen. They were obsidian soot-painted ivory. For her, things are very black and white. She is aware of the complexities of peoples' minds, but she believes that you either love someone or you don't. They mean more than others, or they don't. Things are true or false. Forever or never. All or nothing.

She is beginning to concentrate on herself, for her own internal anxieties and the individuals around her have affected almost everything she has done. If he meant what he said when they were talking, then she will consider the idea of future chances, but the candle has been burned. The lighter is shot. Why she still cares even after the damage, she doesn't know.

She had been aching for relief, but she is now finished. Whatever love was there was arguably a lie. His mistake, not hers. It's feasible that he deemed a rain check to be acceptable or appropriate. Perhaps he feared the words of which she spoke, or he feared her inevitable flight. Perhaps he wanted to free her from the pain. The chances she gave him were likely her folly or delicacy, for taking into account that the judgmental verdict of

himself absolves no "nocent," they were undeserving. She must begin to

heal. She must learn to stop picking at her scabs and stitches.

He finally gave up. She feels as though she has ruined it all, but this

could also be a blessing. He made her world wearier, screwing her over and

sucking her dry. She still stands; she has not broken. She knows that she

wasn't perfect. She never fully let him in. Her heels have hardened, her skin

thick from running and running. Running from herself won't succor. She is

rubbing her skin away, attempting to rip the lips he kissed, tear the cheeks

he brushed, and open her mouth to give him a piece of her mind. She begs

the sun to shine so brightly, that all of her is forgotten. Her falling hair

wraps around her neck, choking her almost as much as the thought of

allowing someone to touch her.

When the love had yet to bleed her dry, she found no need for a

partner's validation. She had accepted solitude, naturally an independent,

reserved individual. When someone exhibited attraction and affection for

her, she postulated the possibility of someone seeing her as a beautiful individual. He did, or so she wanted to believe. She assumed his love was merely desperation. She kept her guard up, but he found a way in, through manipulation, infatuation, and affirmation. He said she was gorgeous, more attractive than anyone else he'd seen. He fell for her and her idiosyncrasies (so he claimed), though she remained cautious. She posited his happiness above hers; that was the character she embodied. It appeared innocent, prior to his manipulation, sexual coercion, codependency, and love bombing. She made an effort to ignore rufous-red flags. She desired love; to be loved. Every person in her life had hurt her. She strained to trust him.

He shattered that trust, yet to an extent, she reciprocated his feelings. She was trapped inside her head for the majority of the relationship, remaining partially detached. She required space and distance. She'd sit silently through attacks of intense anxiety and throbbing. In due course, the disrespect and pain caused by him worsened. The effects of the relationship exceeded the actions of others. She concealed her mental hindrances and affairs well, but she stood up when his triggering and disrespectful behavior induced panic. She was strong and chose to walk away. She was a lover, but she had to leave. Her fondness faded, the pain remaining the only emotion regarding the situation. She didn't break.

He continued to contact her following the termination. When he played dead, she helped him, though he had trapped her. She cut the vines that tethered them together. He told her she was everything. Her repulsion and anxiety heightened, piloting her to request the ceasing of contact.

He didn't deserve her presence. Over time, the triggers were further intertwined with him, and her obsessions and compulsions grew inflamed. Her sexual assault PTSD magnified. She was suffocating; in hell. Her control over her own mental state disappeared. Her strength couldn't preserve control. Her OCD attacked her brain; voices nagging her to "fix" herself, her past, and her mistakes. Her internal response to the ache and loss of control was the exasperation of current obsessions and compulsions. Nothing was "just right," she felt utterly ugly and disgusting.

She never wanted to speak to him again and managed to entirely let go for several months, but wound up contacting him due to photograph-related fixations and distress. His misleading demeanor suggested that he cared, telling her that he wanted to be supportive. She wanted to remain kind and pondered the possibility of him changing. She was over him, but couldn't stop herself from caring about him.

He wasn't over her, and her vulnerability caused her to form brief, fleeting feelings. She was aware of her worsening mental state. Her brain kept attacking, whispering crisp lies into the drums of her ears. She was fearful and hurt. The compulsions, obsessions, and everything was severe enough that while her career, social life, and artistic world remained on track, it was necessary to cut him off once again.

He repeatedly asked her to stay, to try. She tried, but her "need to say" OCD, her "just right" OCD, the pain, caused her to voice hurtful things she didn't wish to say. The triggers were too anxiety-inducing and each time he would say it would work, she needed to shut him down with a painful comment, stealing the smallest drop of hope. She couldn't love him like before. She couldn't trust him. He hadn't changed. She didn't want this to be all about OCD. She wanted to be able to talk about other things. She is deep and psychological. She wished he would never have hurt her.

The photograph obsessions heightened along with body-change fixations. She needed to be as underweight as she was a child, to erase the periods of time of which she despised. Her BMI was below 17 or 16. Now she has maintained a 16.4-17 BMI and continues to try and fix "before." She views her underweight self as fat and swollen. She needed to not be fat. She needed to always be thin. People tell her that she was always thin, but she can't believe it, just like she couldn't tell herself she was clean after three showers or that her face isn't a rat, or that she isn't coated in urine. She is too fused with the lies OCD tells her. She was distorted, she was confused, and aching. She wanted to go back. Back to before. She wanted to erase the triggers, the pain, and the experiences. She wanted to fix things. She developed a branch of relationship OCD and extreme doubt of ever being loved. Although her academic and artistic success was not affected, texting as well as undoing and redoing compulsions took over. She could manage, but she suffocated in her OCD lies, discomfort, and anxiety. Like a broken record, she repeatedly told him to let her go.

He was a trigger for her PTSD, in addition to an OCD trigger. He was pushy, well aware of her sexual past. She asked him to stop responding and feeding her compulsions. The pain was too much, but the voices in her head contradicted her needs, forcing her to keep texting. He had an ulterior motive motivating him to keep talking. He enjoyed their conversation. He told her he would "spend his life with her." He told her that he wouldn't love anyone more. He knew she doubted him. He could have meant it. She couldn't pretend that she was the only one that got hurt in the relationship's entirety. It was a complicated situation.

She needed another favor, therefore, her texting compulsions didn't vanish. After explaining the pain, he told her what he knew to be the truth; "She was always thin. She wasn't dirty. She hadn't ruined her life." Unfortunately, he brought up triggering people and events which resulted in further pain. She pulled herself together and stopped texting. She was determined to stop and wait until the favor was done.

She resisted the urge. She didn't contact him until the date they had agreed upon. He didn't respond. He didn't do the one thing she needed in order to let go of the time of her life that she so desperately wanted to escape. His failure to assist her exacerbated her daily compulsions, habitual hygiene routines, avoidance, and panic attacks. It couldn't possibly be worse. She was getting lost within her OCD and her confusion between reality and not.

She was upset, spearheading obsessive amounts of contact. She was strong and has made it through, failing to give up. While she believes that she is the ugliest creature, she is marching on. The hell he put her through, the misery, still haunts her, whether she talks to him or not. She was holding onto the hope that he really did love her, for she cared, and he was the only one who wanted to be with her. She kept the good in her head. He either loved her so much that he was willing to do what was best for her and lessen the pain, or it was all a lie. The uncertainty doesn't sit well with her. It doesn't matter how either of them feel about each other. It was really the end. She realized she didn't want it to be the end. She wanted to try. Every "toxic" thing he had done, was to get closer to her. She hadn't been able to talk to her mother and her brother, so she thought maybe not talking to him was just a fallout of the OCD. She wanted to push through the pain. If he ad really meant what he said, then she would try. Even the individuals who

urt her and destroyed every ounce of self-esteem or appreciation, have

ove. They are loved, they feel loved, they have left it all behind. She knows

hat one wouldn't have hurt her as they did, if they truly loved her as much

s they claimed. He still held on to others too. It must have been a lie; a lie

hat she was the one or worthy. She could no longer lie to herself. He never

eserved another chance, for love is infatuation, respect, care, and

cceptance. If love was ever there, she knew it had vanished. She felt as

hough she was unlovable.

She swallowed the vision of him with a bottle in his hand, watching

he ring. Was there an alibi for no reply? It was for the best. He had finally

one what she had asked. This is what she said she wanted. She was

pologetic for everything she had done wrong, of every word, every action,

verything. It wasn't what she wanted.

Her anxiety tormented her. She began to experience flashbacks and

elusions. She wasn't better yet. She contacted him to clarify if he was

lanning to attend an event at the school that she is graduating from, and he had left. He didn't respond. She texted excessively, out of anxiety and pai

She was still triggered and as she texted more and more, she felt more

ashamed. He didn't respond, and he didn't even deserve the internal work

she had done, in order to speak to him. He didn't deserve the fact that she

had changed her mind and was willing to try. She didn't want to hurt him.

She was so sorry that she hurt him by repeatedly telling him it would neve

work and that she didn't want that. She was confused, in pain, and now sh

is too late. It didn't count. She tried to believe that he meant what he said,

but deep down she knew that he didn't care anymore. She fell out of love

because of pain, not lack of interest or care. The harm he caused was the

reason she couldn't stay and prevented her feelings from totaling to his. H

told her she was too late. He didn't care anymore. He found someone. He

had told her she was everything, but she believes that he now sees her as

nothing, that it was all fake. He had begged her to stay, but now she finall

wanted to forgive, to push through, and to be there for him. He didn't care

Even when she was hurting, when she was nauseous, when she was

fainting, shaking, triggered, she still cared about his well-being and his happiness. He knew she was having a difficult time, and he chose to be rude. He chose to hurt her one last time. He could have just said he didn't want to speak anymore. Of course, he had options, she never did. She felt unlovable. She felt idiotic. She was still hurting from the original relationship. She will forget it. She will try. She knew she should have kept it in her head like everything else.

She wanted to believe that he had meant what he said. She wanted to believe that he was tired, but didn't stop loving. She let her pain, her OCD, her past, get in the way of her health. What he took from her, she never wants back. She refused to let anyone in completely. When they tried to get close, she left. People got tired; tired of the sensitivity, the silence, the leaving, the distance, the chase. These are not excuses, but merely explanations for habit. She was trying to protect herself and others.

She doesn't want to ever know if he falls in love with someone else. It will hurt too much, even if she isn't in love right now. She can understand that people will have multiple partners, or that he will need to move forward, but she secretly wanted to have the notion in her head that they would always love each other, maybe more than anyone else. When she loves, she never stops.

She cared, and she pushed through the pain to talk to him, even if it was just for a few extra weeks at a time. He had the audacity to respond to her push and pull with remorseless harm and damaging demeanor. Even when it hurt her, she was there when he really needed to be, and he wasn't in the same way. She couldn't stay because his voice, his scent, everything but his eyes, induced the vivid memory and feeling of something inside of her.

Poison Plants-people are triggers too

An African daisy mirrors the powdered mauve

beneath your feathered, dark-amber lashes.

Carolina allspice tongue hugging the back of your teeth,

Dalmatian Iris eyes swelling as my hand leaves your chest.

Every felted curl clings to my gelid fingers,

freezing your flamingo flesh. My skin is a

golden cholla, stabbing you until you gasp for air.

Hemlock swims through my bitter blood.

I'm drowning, and it's too late now. I'm dust.

Jacob's ladder petals are as pale as my enameled skin.

King's mantle knuckles with apricot-orange

lily freckles appear at night as you

make me shiver, and I hug my pitted stomach.

Neoregelia ink is redder than my heart,

obsidian black bleeds on my cheeks,

and Prussian Blue ink seeps into my veins.

Quietly decaying, you let me break,

rotting like a black carrion, tissue scraped raw by your

stippled stubble and by byzantine blackberry

thorns. I need to heal. I can't forget or

undo, but I can ask you to let me go.

Vanilla orchid syrup and mint still coat my lips. I'm barely breathing.

Wishing on wishbone flowers to forget you, like a

Xeranthemum, bubblegum sea urchin, I shut you out.

Yellow bells grow alongside desaturated lemons, the

zest licking my wounds. Like sipping whiskey from the bottle, it burns.

Leach love

Aching lovesick bones are skinned raw,

burning like amaranth flames of abandonment.

Coercive rituals beget fruit fly indignity.

Drunken leeches suck venom from tender veins.

Endoparasitoids drain delicate arms

for stolen luminescence and luster.

Grasshoppers hide in ankleugging grass with vanilla orchids, and

opters crawl on a glowing

llyfish; the mauve stinger, inferior to olive beauty.

isses were ticks embedded into

ght, patina-shellacked tissue,

erely smoked-ash varnish to conceal

eurotic propensity. Days are turned into

donota dancing nights with the strength of black heron wings.

laying dead like Livingstone's cichlids,

uivering lips trace the purple peel of a

vishing goddess.

hapeless moats set to sink skin beetles bear

e antidote to sickly saccharine,

ndying poison; force-fed candied guilt.

ile maggots submerged in custard and spit

ake to nibble at spinal tissue, leaving nothing but

anthic, bulging bumps like

yellow bellies or shielded hills, clouded by disappearing

zigzag ghosts who vacillate and vamoose.

She neurotically craved relief from the pain and the tension, begging

for alleviation. Her languishing heart was eaten alive by fixation, duress,

and bemused love. The sap dampening her eyes crystalized while gaping

stifling strains. She wanted to be seen, to be beautiful. She knelt, imitating

the menage. She was and is wise, but a mooncalf in the name of love.

Even if it is presumed otherwise, she invariably puts others, if not

above, on a plane commensurate to herself. This can be admirable or

abrogating. She could be correct or incorrect about the ones who are gone.

Would one comfort the other if the sun disappeared, the moon faded, the

trees fell, the seas dried up, voices choked, and birds fell, or would it be

exiguous?

It wasn't what she thought, nor what she favored. He thought it was

nothing to her, but as it all unfolded, she reaped that it was even less to him.

After grasping that in its entirety, it meant nothing, so she could morph the experience into anything she desired. She once loved optimism and her imagination, but that love disappeared for a few years. She loathed false hope, imaginary happiness, or "pretending." Now she can see the brightness within memory and imagination. It can transport someone from a world saturated with anxiety and pain into a new one. Naturally, everyone comes back to reality. She shouldn't have taken the hope away from him, for she used to squirm at the delusion of him, but now she forces it. She is still holding on, for the nightingale that she thought was an angel, the one that sheds its disguise and revealed its devil core, was the best thing she ever held.

It was as if he stabbed her, and she apologized for the bleeding. She will still apologize for it. She will apologize for how she responded to the pain he caused. How she responded to the triggers. In the end, she left him knowing she did it all for him, and he left her knowing or possibly believing that she is nothing. There is still so much she would say to him, and yet nothing at all. It would be a crime for her to reach out, so she resists. She resists for him. She resists the urge, even the compulsion. She has fought the chemicals. Her pain doesn't matter anymore.

A story

"I suppose it's too late. I am shivering in the sun, the light filtering through my window seams; the same rays that caress abutting apartment complexes. I grip the iris wallpaper dressing the walls. My hands and back feel like velvet against the spider-eggplant, marble tile. My soaked flesh is spongy, like a used tissue kissing my bones. The bathtub is half full of soap. The eyes of my spine are bruised sandpaper-yellow and steel-blue. Cool air seeps through the crack in the wall above the toilet. A toilet covered in grime, on top of a floor covered in dirt, in a room filled with germs, in a house full of filth, surrounding a disgusting body. My nails are tinted and my tips are pruned, as I finger the patches of raspberry and cantaloupe, enameled to my skin. As I stand, my knees crack like the crunching of a boot, on a chocolate beetle. I stand naked in front of her mirror, varnished by fingerprint oil.

Staring at my reflection, I reach for one of the four mascara tubes in the cabinet above the paper-white sink. My lashes are coated in matte black

Duchess-red lipstick licks my teeth as I bite my bottom lip. I stare into the mirror as though my eyes don't recognize the woman before me. I squint my eyes and walk through the rather scratched door frame, prancing down the carpeted staircase.

At the last step, the carpet changes from a bone-white triexta to an alabaster polyester. The carpet stretches to the crisp edge of the still. I step outside and a car horn barks. I glance at the bench at the edge of the sidewalk, the frost on the grass, the smoke shop straight ahead, and the toy store across the street. As I approach the crosswalk, I look up at the traffic lights. I watch the light turn red and close my eyes, picturing the moment I thought everything was going to be ok.

I remember the night he stood under an imperial red, bar exit sign. The E and T were dead, and the moon had yet to chase the saffron sun away. He rested his back against a streetlight post, chewing on his nails and spitting them out, like gum that's lost its taste. Bluebird veins kissed his wrists, capering around cinnamon skin sprinkle freckles.

I was claustrophobic, trapped in a trunk, a child with cat scratches on her back, a girl with waves in her brain, a woman in pain, but I was strong. I wasn't a doll, but maybe I wanted to be. I sat tall with my painted face and decorated fingers. I glanced at the man in front of the bar, from the cold metal bench at the edge of the curb. I traced the ridges next to my right thigh. I saw him in the dark, kicking pure air as if it were a rusty, used can or a soccer ball. He approached me slowly, silently sitting down beside me. I rose from the bench and attempted to walk away. I stared at the dirt on the ground, with cracks in my cheeks, a knife in my heart, a pit in my stomach, and a tumor in my brain. I didn't know that my porcelain body was going to shatter.

He doesn't smoke, but in my mind he does, for I felt like a cigarette. He looked at the scales on his callus hands and hugged my fragile neck. He reached into his iron-shadow jeans, feeling around for his lighter. He pulled out a silver manual zippo, holding it in his right hand. A couple of men walked out of the bar and chuckled. He paused for a second. He looked at em and then at his own body, as though he was comparing. As their voices

rew fainter as they moved further away, my Turkish gold lungs turned

arlet. He scratched his nose as the torrid hair tickled his cartilage.

My skin was burning. He sucked me dry. With his lips, he coated my

ody. He painted it with spit, and he tossed me to the ground. I didn't want

is. The rubber soles on his shoes crushed my core, as he stomped on my

ones. Saliva webbed from sticky mead, like tiger marigold honey,

wallowing my heart within. He peered through the window of the pub and

atched people attempting to drown out their worries, filling shot after shot,

lass after glass. Wine blood drowned my muscles, bumblebee crust clung

 my paper skin. I had begun to disintegrate, becoming the ash that stings

is fingertips. We both suffocated. My body was now burnt trash on the

avement. He stared at me and sighed, before crossing the street.

He was supposed to save me. Instead, he broke me more than

efore. He took a broken girl and suffocated her. Maybe we shouldn't have

net, but without him, I would still believe I was ugly. I can't go back. He is

ot the sun. My world spins on its own. He can't undress me again. He is a speck of dust in a filthy world. I am not porcelain. I am made of steel.

My boots glide across the cement, skipping each painted white line on the street. There it was. The seaweed metal bench, with finger-sized holes in the seat; holes big enough for granulate and powder candy to jump through. I clutch my handbag and my half-full bottle, an assorted mix of Klonopin, Sertraline, and Advil rattles. I need 12 pills a day now, but even that's not enough to fight myself, to forget the taste of licorice Listerine and yellow kumquats, to forget his face, to ignore my obsessions, to stop my compulsions, to quiet the noise. I wish I could quiet the noise.

I reach my ghostly-pale hand into my peach fuzz purse. The plastic beaded bracelet on my narrow wrist catches on the black felt mask, sleeping with weathered receipts and tarnished coins. Ignoring the dampened lining of my bag, I pull out my translucent, orange bottle, and swallow my pills like tapioca pearls. I just wait. It fails to relieve me of the water trapped in my lungs. I race to her door, to the bathroom, to the shower, shedding my clothes, and lathering my body in cups of soap. The water heats quickly.

Water streams down my reddening back and pulsating stomach. My skin and bones are washed raw as my eyes grow blurry. My forehead rests against the eggplant tile. The gurgling of water in the metal drain reminds me of his voice. The darkening of my wet hair matches the color of my swollen pupils. Soap and water swim into my ears. Maybe if I grew deaf, it would quiet the noise."

She deserves respect. She deserves to forget. Another Valentines, another number, another year, another age, another burnt-bouquet birthday, with despairing candy hearts. The chocolate tastes like soil and the candles drip like white, salted tears. She stands in a tight dress, composed, not a mess. She knows that she will most likely roll in her grave, unable to let the past go. It was time to let it all go; let the passing of stations function as moments or memories that she must leave behind.

What if it never changes? What if it does?

Can he still taste it?

Can she?

He creeps into her mind. She scolds herself for the unwanted thoughts of the past. Memories make healing difficult. Every place, every correlation, his name, his scent, his face, his voice, her face, and the places he's touched; they are all triggers.

It's over, it's in the past, it was temporary. Right? She begs the moon, "please make them forget about me," in defiance of the shaking, the cramp, and the repulsion. She doesn't want to let it fade into nothingness. She can't un-love. She never wanted them to fall in love with someone else. She knew that they'd find someone better. She told them. She knows they did. She asked for too much. She does not care if people tell her it wasn't love. It was. She knows it was just not enough love.

Apparently, her PTSD, her anxiety, her pain, her fear, and her repulsion haven't stopped her from caring. She only ever wanted to make people and him happy. He saved her in the end, though. He finally let go. Her pain turned to lust and desire, and then hate and relief, until it led to more pain. It pains her to think of all that she is sorry for. She wishes she could have pushed through. She wishes she could have endured the triggers the PTSD, and the pain for longer. She wishes she was better. She knows that no matter her location, her career, her future, in two years, in five years, in ten years, in 40; she will drop everything. She won't renege on the last thing she told him.

Ironically, the ones who hurt her the most were the only ones who ever had any impact on how she viewed herself. They were the ones that made her question her self-doubts, but they fractured her self-worth. Those people were strangled and choked like a dog in a collar.

The OCD took him and tangled both of them up in a knot. If she were bereft of the obsessions and compulsions, distance would be sensible, nevertheless. It took others as well. It took her brother first, then him, then her mother. Loss without absence is acetic.

Is sour cold or hot?

Parrot

Match

She walked

through hell

for a man

she wanted

to give

everything to.

She gave up

everything she loved.

He set a match

and she spent

so much

time trying

to put the

fire out.

She thought

the fire

would burn

them down.

What if

that fire

was a spark?

What if

those memories

are now ash?

What if

the flame

was supposed

to burn forever?

How did they

end up here?

Now she's burning

all alone.

Speaking and silence

are the same.

The pain

and the burning

don't grow

or die.

The pain remains.

The good and bad

will remain.

There is certainty and uncertainty regarding the emotion, opinions,

or actions of another. That uncertainty is either accepted or scrutinized.

Humans doubt themselves and their abilities. Concerns about relationships, decision-making, character, and control are ordinary, but when pervasive and persistent, doubt can expose the severity of suffering. One may focus on their perceived truth rather than understanding that a sense of reality can be tacit. A feeling of certainty or uncertainty, while possibly tacit and implicit, is a necessity. The constituents of existential feelings offer a horizon in which things and ideas can appear. Illness reveals one's relationship with their body and bodily feelings. Radical modification of a body or its experience is largely concealed, like a head, patent under a river of rocks.

Are the actions, the people, the affairs in front of her perceived similarly by the mass traveling inside the train car?

A restless little girl kicks her legs, like a pair of scissors, pointing her satin-enveloped toes downward. Her tiny fingers pick at her blush tights as she hums. The little dancer reminded her of when she was young. Her grandmother; her mother's mother, the one with the cottage and property, would accompany her to weekly ballet classes. She can still taste the peppermint on her tongue, from the peppermint candies offered at the ballet studio.

Marzipan and cherry leotards,

fire and butterfly capes,

braided hair, ruby ribbons,

blush, leather, crimson toes,

brick stages, burgundy curtains,

compressed intestines, pumping blood,

raw rouge skin, protruding bones,

ice backs, maroon lips, rose scleras,

nutcrackers cracking hearts.

All the pain floods

for applause, for worth, and for beauty.

She reminisces about the dancing, the candies, her grandmother, and
the cottage. She recalls the small performances she would put on by the
fireplace; the songs she would sing with her sister, the improvised dances,
the spoken poetry. She grew shy quickly. Perhaps that is why her art is
rather independent, perfected in the preparation, rather than a performance.
She prefers independence.

When she contemplates her introversion, she often follows the ribbons that tie her to family members. Her grandmother, on her mother's and the one on her father's line, are very different. Their personalities are quite a contrast of character. Her father's mother is sociable, traditional, and lighter. Her mother's mother is complex, strange, a wallflower. She is one that has others, but not many. She requires space, like her mother's mother. She can be isolated and difficult, but she is caring. They both hold a lot of love.

She wants to go back to the cottage. She wants to go through the objects, the clothing, the furniture, everything. She wants to understand her roots. She, unlike her mother, will not become what she came from. She knows what she dislikes and what has hurt her. She will not repeat. She will not harm. She doesn't want to.

A man uses a rainbow-plume, ornate, whittled cane, to doddle to his seat. His blistered hands are intertwined above the legs of his blue and white striped suit. His cranberry shirt correlates with his leather briefcase. He takes a plastic bag of caramels and sour candies from his briefcase. It's peculiar for a man his age to be carrying candy, let alone sour-dusted ones.

"Would you like a piece?" he asks, offering one to the woman beside her.

"What?" she asks, removing a frayed earbud wire from her ear.

"Do you want a piece?"

"Oh," she chuckles, "I'm fine."

"Would you like one?" he asks the little girl next to the woman.

"Yes," she exclaims. "My favorite is the green apple and the lemon."

"Really?" he asks, sounding intrigued.

"My mom says that they are the ones that most mature people like."

"Oh, I see."

"I like acquired tastings."

"Do you like licorice?"

"It depends." "Sometimes it's good, but sometimes it's gross."

"It can be intense."

"Yeah, like vinegar is sometimes good."

"Vinegar?"

"Yeah."

"Vinegar isn't candy."

"I know," she exclaims.

our

asts of acrid juices chafe.

inegar has a sour intensity.

iting sap glazes

amed scabs and

ozen muscles.

he heat from a head,

om a nose, and a mouth

eutralize the

ost of a pomelo.

ongues drool for

gar and honey,

ust and bones

are cremated into candy soil

like the insides of

kumquats, and lips

lick saccharine-touched corpses.

The red and pink turn gray

like the smoke of the red moon;

not blue. Blue is cold, or so one would infer,

but the heart of a flame; the hottest of hots

is blue; blue like veins and irises.

Blue turns to yellow like

sweet-lime calamansi.

Tears run clear

after the boiling and

the draining of black,

running rivers from the eye.

They search for

wild fur and miss

purple martian hats.

Fingers dig for mauves and

yellows like strong lemons;

colors of the royals

and of polarity.

Sweet, spicy, bitter,

sour.

Sour like the milk

of animals;

animals that die

with each word,

each step, each call.

The animals inside

are the shadows that hang

heavy like a cold chill.

A sour intensity.

Intense like red, purple, yellow,

orange, or like flames.

Not blue. Blue is soft.

Red is sticky, purple is pure, yellow is bright,

orange is heavy, and white is suffocating.

Purple, green, red, brown, black. Black is anxious

and intense; it feels cold but comforting.

A sour tongue is hot against a chilled body.

Hot, Cold, Bitter, Sour.

A woman cups a half-peeled tangerine. White pieces of the stringy

sleeve inside the rind fall to the floor. They float quickly but don't disappear

The skin makes its way back; to air, to the ground. It's like dust, or the

glassy taste of coming; like thick lungs, like syrup, like paint.

Palette

Her palette is comprised of an orderly arrangement of colors. It is

composed of both vivid and desaturated hues.

Abalone like Brumous

Ash like tenebrose

Burnished-amber like sugar

Blood like Artuate

Cedar like feuillemort

Cantaloupe like Haihtuu

Daffodil like phosphenes

Gold like foxing

Lime-lapis like amity

Mint like selcouth

Dark-green like growth

Silver like petrichor

Teal-salamander like

Tiffany like Ruby and Ramé

Ultraviolet like drowning

Ube like cafuńe

Wisteria-heather like sweven

Wine-Salmon like meat

White like lacuna

Zebra like blackened contradiction

She used to be a painter. She is a painter. She has always had a keen sense of color and beauty. She analyzes the aesthetic, persona, and quiddity of those around her. Each person she encounters is a distinct shade or compound of color, based solely on first impressions. Their colors may darken, fade, brighten, or drastically transform.

The dark and bright ones are the people she gravitates towards. They are frequently the ones who are unhealthy or overly intense. The individuals that she dislikes are predominantly pastels, and pastels are almost universal. She allows for a budding development of an appreciation for the bijou of pastel colors, through embracing diversity and courtesy. The superlative pastels; yellow abricity and moon-blue, are serene and sensible. For them, admiration grows with time. People with earthy, gritty, or organic hues are the ones that discern her.

Her friends are generally vibrant or musky. They are like rainbow birds. Her loves are aromatic. Her lust is frequently noticed amongst a combination of purple and honey. She appreciates purple but despises orange. Perhaps she is attracted to people because of their colors, or perhaps their dyes are determined by her reverence or fondness.

She is scrupulously darker, manifesting an array of jewel tones. Sometimes within herself, her complexion and color dissipate, becoming invisible. Either the colors vanished, or she encouraged them to. Colors are similar to flavors. Colors and flavors can be dull, bland, soft, harsh, cool, warm, vibrant, or intense. Intensity can be both positive and negative. Occasionally, it's ideal for colors, flavors, people, places, everything, to be diluted or washed away.

Flamingo

She is graceful, delicate, and elegant, like a pink bird that stands on one leg. Her curls are brown, but her fluff is dyed pink from the food she eats. Her mind feeds her concentrated lies. Her mouth swallows plastic pasta, lavender dental floss, and heavy-syrup peaches. She brushes her teeth with fire, and she grooms herself in alkaline lakes or serene estuaries. She stands on one leg, balancing, despite the push and pull of the water lapping against her frozen feet. The current is still one moment and wild the next, like sudden rushes of color. The bark of her body is tough and red, like the reddest of redwoods; like velvet darkness. She freezes and flees, but she does fight. She has never been aggressive, but she knows herself and her desires.

She needed to get away, so she went back to the whitewashed cottage. Her wild imagination led her to make her own assumptions about the people who have been inside the house or on that property. She considered the land and animals, who first owned the house, who lived there, the guests, the family, friends, group members, and the current emptiness.

Inside the house, she sat at the glass, rounded kitchen table, and stared at the bowl of figs. She eyed the spider crawling up a strawberry-bat mug and her lace burgundy bra, hanging above a twine bag of pomegranates. The pomegranates sat beside a china sugar bowl, a rain-soaked basket of picked blueberries, tinted bottles and jars filled with heart-shaped stones and freshly picked flowers, a jewel-tone teapot, and a cherry branch. She sipped an iced vanilla latte with almond milk, out of a pink-rimmed rhubarb glass.

Pink

I'm following a peach-pink jeep,

hoping it'll lead me back;

back to a space where

everything was in its place.

I held on to a presence.

You in the physical

are the equivalence of sickness.

You are pain, but I thought

I could hold onto

an idea, a notion.

An idea shouldn't induce a shiver.

You shouldn't sting

if you can't even touch me.

You repulse me.

You dress me like dirt.

I wasn't in my body,

down on earth,

yet when I wanted to forget,

when I hated the colors of your face,

still wanted you all to myself.

wanted love.

wanted candy hearts

and roses;

roses like the ones

shoved into the jeep.

The jeep is pink

like your pink lips, your pink tongue,

and your pink hands.

Everything is pink.

Petals are pink.

You gave me flowers once;

flowers that rotted, wilted, and died.

Everything you touch breaks;

my cheek, my bones, and my composure.

I was bleeding and aching.

You took the dead flowers and watered them

in an attempt to regrow what you killed.

Flower bouquets dangle

out of the open trunk.

Petals have melted to a license plate.

The plastic sleeve turned to glue.

You held on. I tried to let go.

I don't want the love to fade,

to lessen, or to disappear.

I think you are tired.

hink you have let your hope

de into the night

ke an orange-yellow sun.

is yellow like your yellow-purple palette.

is orange like your favorite color.

am stuck in a swamp of confusion;

uick sand of contradictory.

don't want you in reality,

the physical,

the now, in the future.

want the idea,

e promise, the love,

nd the memories, but I want to forget.

very tiny flower

minds me of you.

You told me you loved me.

Maybe you still do.

In the end, I hope

I never see you again,

yet I'm following a pink jeep.

It may lead me to you.

I should stay away.

I should have

stayed away.

I need to stop.

I should stop reading

the tiny words;

the script finely printed

on newspaper that is wrapped

around bouquets of flowers.

The gloved stems weaken,

rotting,

pressed against

the hot trunk.

The plastic blurs the text.

I will never let

myself get too close.

I maintain a 3,4,7 second

following distance between myself

and the pink jeep.

I know love and life

are not all or nothing.

It may not be all or nothing,

but it's now or never.

I can't decide.

I don't know.

Do I like pink?

As she watched the pink jeep drive out of sight, she plodded through

a field of dandelions. She saw the young, yellow sprouts as children, and

saw the gray, fluffed poms as mothers. The mother is the one that grants

wishes and heals, but it blows away. The babies collect dust and bones as

the mothers turn to ash and abandon them. They either die young, fail to

provide what they need, or both. Dandelions are wistful. They are like

fairies. They dance, like fairies in the sky or jellyfish in the sea.

She is similar to a fairy, but in high contrast to a jellyfish;

A creature that glows, that's bright, that's warm.

She is dark, cold, intense, and comforting.

A jellyfish has no eyes, no bones, no brain, no heart.

She is kind, her eyes see beauty, see ugly, see pain.

Her brain knows right, knows wrong, knows knowledge.

Her heart loves, her heart aches, her heart bleeds.

Her bones break, her bones shatter.

Her bones hold her high, her bones are strong.

A jellyfish does not feel.

A jellyfish does not remember.

She feels immensely.

She remembers everything; remembers too much.

A jellyfish is flexible, it does not think.

She overthinks and overanalyzes.

She doesn't like change.

She sat at the glass table and looked through the clouded window.

She saw a couple of cranes nipping at frogs hiding in the grass.

Polluted ability

Prairie cranes lick contaminated lizards and frogs.

Polluted topsoil coats rich rinds with specks.

Soda cans and black ribbons sleep on gravel sand.

The grains of elastic skin are clogged

with uncomfortable honey.

It's like heavy-syrup peaches on a toothbrush.

Pallid cheeks are stroked with thumbs.

Rose petal pets are bumpy and

feel like chiseled starvation.

Pokes and brushes are

cacti piercings in

azure hail.

Feet are cold, frozen to cement.

Shoulders are shaking under

hood that is ripping under the seams.

ick has broken down.

itched barriers come undone

e a stocking with runs.

ere is nowhere to run

to hide.

is time to give in.

andles still flicker in the dark,

raid of their own hearts.

ey remember their burn.

nce they melt,

ey can never stretch as far.

hey are restrained and contained.

Memories live in dreams,

people live in nightmares.

Every person prevents restful sleep.

Nightmares choke a child

like a child drowns

a self-caught pet frog.

Three monsters behind

a bed frame.

Monsters or imaginary friends.

The line between imagination and

delusion is thin as the glass

between sane and insane or love and hate.

People can only move forward,

ignore the monsters; the predators.

Occasionally, they can travel back.

Some can fly backward like a hummingbird.

Hummingbirds can fly backward.

It can be a benediction or a curse.

She continues to admire the behavior and manner of the cranes; the way they interact with the plants, the water, the dirt, berries, leaves, the frogs, the lizards, the eagles, and the foxes.

Birds are powerful or powerless. They are primary consumers or herbivores. Some are high, and some are low on the food chain; birds of prey versus seedlings. Birds are similar to humans, in the context of; serving as food. Humans are rarely eaten, but rarely dangerous to bigger, wilder mammals.

Animals are either predators or prey. Predators; organisms that hunt and kill are carnivores and omnivores. Predators use camouflage, venom, superior strength, biological characteristics, and speed to catch prey. Prey are not weak. Being consumed is inevitable unless one is hidden. Hiding is difficult amongst an exposed world. The ultimate desires are safety, freedom, and comfort. Some preys are just bait. One example is minnows. Minnows never grow old, for they don't get the chance. They are merely bait. Some animals are deemed worthy of something other than a seat in the circular food chain. What makes a creature purely food? Emotion, feeling, character, size? Would you rather be the hunter or the prey?

Animals are eaten, or they die of age. They are swallowed by the growth and decay of the ground. All living things decay; decay like molded bread, fuzzy fruits, browning leaves, and inverted, shriveled flesh. It can be ugly, but it can also be beautiful, like ruin, rust, or experience.

Death, decay, rot; imprints pigment residues: pretty, concentrated stains. The surface; the skin; it's a blood pool. Its swimmers are permanent residents; words, events, memories, aches of silence. The marks of rot are associated with loss, decay, and endings. On occasion, rot is positive. It spawns regrowth, evolution, and positive change. Sometimes, it's a reminder of a collapsed world. A loud, or a silent, still world. Still, still, still. Everything is still. It is still until it's gone; gone in minutes. Gone in minutes, like orange scattered skies; the skies that shout mandarin and spice.

She hates orange. She hates orange, but she loves her rust skirt. Her own desires, her own needs, her own mind, they contradict themselves. Her ability to control herself varies. She can effectively control herself and her reactions, particularly when other people are involved. If the matters she wishes to control are solely affecting herself, she may find it increasingly difficult to rationalize her ideas, feelings, thoughts, or actions.

When she is stressed, she loses her ability to be present and experience what is happening around her. She periodically travels within her mind, which can be confusing, distressing, or simply an illusion. She dissociates occasionally. She can't control all of her pictured images or situations that have been constructed within her brain. At times, she is subconsciously controlling fictitious characters or situations.

An example of her control complications is a pair of plastic gloves.

When she visualizes intertwined plastic gloves, though the image is created by her own mind, they cannot be separated, even if she wants them to. She also attempts to control scenarios within her mind; a conversation, an event, or an assumed personality of someone around her.

The scenarios aren't always voluntary. Scenarios may be realistic or completely insane, but they have the innate power to change how she feels about ideas or things in reality.

As she sits, fundamentally and intrinsically silent, within her mind, she is moving and speaking. While she is elegantly still, these scenarios are inherently an imitation or phenomenon of her fears or desires. For instance, if she is thinking about herself, people, her family, her home, her houses, the cottage, or the therapy, she could initially begin with a realistic or factual situation, then abandon that idea and begin to envisage the arbitrary or unfeasible. She can be sitting on a train and thinking about a real place, with one or more real people, and then add events, objects, instances, and people that either bring her anxiety or comfort.

While people do strange things, while people change and evolve, emories, core values, pain; it all sticks. Experiences and people remain.

auma, discomfort, and agony can unleash an untamed mind.

   She remembers one picture in particular, from the trunk of objects

d rubbish; a grainy print of a bouquet. That image was real, but her mind

ok the image and morphed it. An image of flowers can prompt an image

wilted roses and petals, and leaves and roots, and bones and skin, and

ir and feathers, and birds and babies, and restraint and cages, and

sentially, a world created from a unique, original human experience.

rhaps that very image could have provoked the idea of beauty, or of

mininity, or gifts, or design. To some, just simple flowers. The wiring of

r brain can either be a cold curse or a warm gift.

Owl

Snowy owl thunder; she heard the thunder of icy white a decade

ago.

Fair white; a cotton sky of the duration of mineral silence. Silence i

broken by falling plaster; sheer skin that has become discolored ash. Crania

bones, a cracked septum; a cadaver waiting in absence. Silent wings

struggle to flap as if they are gossamer armor, slapped with yogurt and

honey. A jaw stretches as it nests hollow, fragile, largish, empty eggs;

hangmen mosaics, ruins of miracles, and velvet resurrection. Stains,

remnants, and fossils; they aren't the bones; they aren't the animal, and they

aren't the essence. They are merely a substance or gritty memory of that

presence. It is never an exact replica of the real thing, like a simulacrum.

She remembers impressions of white. White; a limn of purity,

cleanliness, safety, a new beginning, or peace. White, for her, is uncomfortable, cold, and distant. It looks and feels like pain, like filth, and like death. It's ironic how her least favorite color (shade) shows up everywhere. Milk, ceilings, daisies in the grass, yarrow by the bench, white specks that flavor an escutcheon, manipulating mustache; a cloak above a ruthlessly chubby tongue, tiny white flowers where her old flame begged her to say she loved him, white flowers on his shirt, white flowers on her shirt, white flowers in her hair, white flowers on her shoes, white flowers on the kitchen table, white flakes of dragon skin; from water, from soap, from cream, from scrubbing her stomach, cheeks, her chin, and her chest, oleander on the terrace, jasmine on the door, white walls in a waiting room, white toilets and sinks, white paper, and white flowers on her skirt.

She relives her memories and revisits the flowers. She stares at Yarrow and wishes she had fought harder. She returns to the tiny white flowers and wishes she didn't leave so many times. She examines her clothing, remembering where they came into her possession, what/who she has worn them with, and what words have been spoken. These are reminders of moments that could symbolize the loss of what white was supposed to represent. Notes of celestial sin are now suspended, in the midst of surrounding rubble and the consequences of disorder. Everything or nothing is concerted.

She is prepared for most. She knows her triggers, her reminders, and whether it is appropriate to avoid or face them. Avoidance can either be the safer option, preventing further issues or worsening of triggers, or the anxiety around the avoided subjects can intensify, rather than lessen over time. The act of avoidance can be a compulsion within itself. Her mind can take over, and she can avoid people, places, and even the outdoors (at least in the presence of the sun). Agoraphobia might be sucking at her toes.

When she is on the move, she walks regally, with speed. Her extra small, silk-lined, leather jacket drapes over the blue-purple veins on her forearm. Her complexion is similar to rose eyelids and over-watered, over-cooked pasta. The keratin and tissue clinging to her bones have been under too much stress and pressure.

She dresses in a tank top and a skirt, but covers her back and shoulders as much as possible, by wearing a coat or jacket. It is extremely hot, and while she is always cold, she is overheating when she keeps the jacket on. So, when she isn't wearing it, she keeps a jacket on her arm or in her canvas tote bag. When she ventures out of the shade, she flips her leather jacket around her shoulders to shield herself from the sun. She sees the smirks and the double takes of people passing by. If she does not shield herself properly or her anxiety gets the best of her, she occasionally remains inside, until the sun goes down and the light evaporates.

In the absence of light, one will fall. One will stumble and hit the bottom harder each time. No one can win the war of absurdity. Strangers can see her getting pulled, dragged into disease. Bubbles pop and rubber bands snap, but she won't break. She will not crumble. It may not be ok, but it's not over. She is not gone yet.

Her mind and her body are strong, even if sometimes it feels as though her body is dehydrated, over-hydrated, drained, exhausted, disintegrating, and wasting away. She is scared that she is rotting, and it's irreversible.

Blood pigeon

She watches as a woman peels a ripened banana. A few years back,

she ate a profusion of bananas. She stares at the now compost trash on the

ground; food that will rot and decay like the remainder of her ebullience.

She had been hurt by a considerable number of people. Her perennial, kind

nature is occasionally lost within remnants of her past.

The people around her, the places, and the objects (the triggering

ones); they all rub her pain, her anxiety, her failures, her imperfections in.

They rub them in like stinging lotion, like poison oak oils, or lime juice in

cuts.

Growing up, her mother, brother, and others had made comments

about her body, appearance, and perceived "flaws." They were critical and

hurtful, sticking with her. Her mother, while well-intentioned, had

exacerbated some of her worries and pain. A mother can protect and soothe r child, but a mother can tear her child apart with a single phrase. Though

e is a good mother, she failed to comfort and assist her when she needed it

e most. She couldn't tell what was true and false with the things that were

id to be OCD. Yes, it isn't always that simple, but it is with these things.

lse or true. Her mother refused to tell her that her obsessive beliefs

eren't true.

She only mentioned the anxiety component, confirming her

rceptions. Her brother, while having caused a great amount of destruction

her self-esteem, undid his damage with a comment that was intended to

negative, but was exactly what she wanted to hear. The only person who

er convinced her that it was all OCD was her ex-lover, whom she can no

nger believe due to the turnout and disbelief in everything he ever said.

e craved comfort and ease. She couldn't and wouldn't deceive herself. She

n't fight the OCD, because she doesn't believe it's all false. Commentaries,

tions, and experiences can all confirm, trigger, invalidate, repair, or

gravate these matters. What engendered the OCD, and when did it begin?

it nature or nurture?

Nature is pre-wired, genetic and biological makeup. It is influenced by inheritance and genetic predisposition. Nurture is broadly perceived as the influence of external factors on an individual after birth, such as the commodity of exposure, upbringings, and acquired knowledge. By blood, gene, and inclination, she is kind, compassionate, and strong, but she is also compulsive and obsessive. She is loving and gentle at heart, so it does not manifest itself in misbehavior, anger, or malice. Her issues and reaction to pain externalize a need for perfection.

Perhaps there is a positive aspect to who she is and has become. She'd be quite different if it weren't for the emotional turmoil and the people she's known. Her experiences are unforgettable, but she has the green-rubber stomach to come back; to grow with the dehydrated green of the plants covered in dirt.

She fights reminders of betrayal and flashbacks of phallic figures before dusk, similar to early flower visits with ruby-throats. There is no betrayal without love. She, too, has sold people down the river. She pushes people away due to fear, but not because she is weak at the knees or vacuumed by a currant. She never wanted to push people away. She didn't want fear, pain, or a feeling of losing control. She doesn't sleep anymore. She can hear the silence where she failed to speak; failed to tell people she loved them. The nurturing, stone-walled her nature. She was trying to be strong. She was trying to protect herself. She didn't want to be a floating fish or a flower-snake eaten by eagles of regret. She isn't. She still stands.

She may be resilient, but she isn't a robot. Sometimes she can't fight her emotions. She is perceived as emotionally calm. She can regulate her feelings, excluding when it comes to her anxiety. She can overreact. When she thinks of emotions and rationality, the line is a little hazy. What is magnification and what is understandable? She used to think of emotions as resembling the idea of giving birth to flowers. In the end, they all die, sitting in vases filled with bacteria-infected liquid. Depending on the emotions' mother, they may be displayed on a kitchen table or by the front door; somewhere commonly populated, or a bedroom stand, or by a bathroom sink; more secluded and concealed.

The emotional buds can be a variety of variants and colors, but they all cause hearts to ache and stomachs to cramp as they mature. Sometimes it's hard to have faith in the ceasing of the pain.

She doesn't think the pain will ever go away. Her fingers twitch, her shoulders shake, and she has begun to see a faded face, hear a faded voice, and feel faded touches. The presence of distant individuals occurs in her dreams. The people that are gone, she will see them again when she falls asleep. She used to, but she hasn't slept in nights. The figures she holds onto are really gone; eyes, arms, and every freckle. The molds of hands cupping her flesh are chipping. Fading is the product of her own disappearance. She ran like the sun, but she came back with the next rise. She "set" too many times. Maybe the sky has banished her from teasing with temporary light.

Shattered-Devil Glass

She shut her eyes,

thinking of what could be

for a brief instant,

mixing reality with fantasy.

Her mind is a purée

of sweet bath tears

and slabs of sulfur-blood

branches that stand erect.

She attempted to flee,

shouting her migration

before her inevitable flight,

despite the known consequences.

She hit devil glass,

now lying on broken tile,

wounded and still

like taxidermy or a doll.

The crash is melting her wings.

The pressure of perception

and exactness lick

her plucked, stripped skin.

Her devoted roses

have been de-coated.

The dust mixes with grime

as the sun gnaws her liquor flesh.

Spit runs through her veins

while pickled plants

urinate on her wounds

and dampen her heated wings.

Dead walk behind her

with unrecognizable faces.

They have left her

with nothing at all.

She is no warmer than the deceased,

for she has a vampire heart.

She is cold,

removed, and distanced.

A vampire is icy,

hidden from the sun,

maintaining a gray

or purple complexion.

Her face is gray and her hands are purple.

Like them, she is not

warm to the touch.

Vampires can be warm, however.

Warmth of others, acceptance,

and love can bring warmth to a vampire.

Vampires are only cool on the exterior.

They are tender-hearted within.

She is resilient,

but her insides,

her organs, and her heart

are freezing.

Like a vampire,

in the mirror,

beyond her stare,

she sees nothing there.

Her eyes may be glassy,

her heart may be torn,

and her arms may be

speckled with goosebumps.

She may appear broken,

but she is not.

She may appear cold,

but she's not. She is strong.

She is practically nocturnal,

from hiding inside until dark.

Night is her hour, and solitude is her comfort.

She is like an owl, perhaps.

She is not blind

with dark distress.

She is finding serenity to accept

he things she can't control.

From behind fragments of fog,

smoldering encroachment

acts as the perfume of the sky,

broadcasting pessimism.

The color of the sky is hardly as bright

as the blue edges

of her marble tongue

and the skeleton remains.

Her delicate frame protects her; her

rose eyelids, her vampire

heart, and her thin,

overcooked-pasta epidermis.

    She is attempting to cut connections and sever associations with

specific objects, places, and people. An external or internal interpretation of an external phenomenon triggers memories. Memories are not replayed instantaneously. She is learning to divert her attention. She feels less and less capable of completing daily tasks and being around others without getting upset. This is causing her to feel confined or constrained.

Through analyzing the root and maturation of her obsessions and compulsions, she was able to identify the triggers for each category of her anxiety, hyper-fixations, and beliefs. Her childhood and her experience growing up in her home with her parents, given the nurture and nature components, formed a piece of who she is today. Each negative event, comment, and belief triggered her distress and anxiety.

Her Obsessive-Compulsive Disorder symptoms; obsessions and compulsions have evolved as a result of traumatic events. Following specific occurrences, her poor self-esteem, the belief that she is unworthy, not perfect enough, ugly, disgusting, dirty, and so on, began. Her current anxieties and beliefs are internal, stemming from subconscious desires or preferred circumstances.

Her lack of self-worth and feeling of being dirty began at a young age. While she has an exceptional memory and can distinctly remember her emotions and perception at the age of 3 or 4, she cannot recall the trigger for her earliest compulsions. One of those compulsions was wearing the same green shirt daily.

She can recognize specific events involving her brother, her neighbors, and her mother that prompted a number of her earlier flare-ups. Her handwriting obsession, need for perfection, hygiene rituals and excessive cleaning, beauty routines, food anxiety, low self-esteem, and depersonalization were all rooted in some situation, comment, thought, or discovery.

While others have had an impact on her, and some believe she is sensitive, she rarely cares what others think of her, as long as she is perceived in the way she wants. She tries to protect her loved ones and ensure that they do not end up with similar issues or pain. She is aware that others' comments and actions have such an impact on her mental health. She wants to shield the ones that she cares about, for example, her sister, who is still a rather cheerful child. She differs greatly from her sister, but she still attempts to prevent what she has experienced.

She knows she has the ability to handle everything, but some people snap more easily or quickly than others. She fought, she suppressed her emotions, and she forgave everyone, but at her core, she still aches. That is something she would never wish on anyone.

Her OCD began to attack as a way to protect and provide false control when she was in a great deal of pain and had no coping strategies. She began to believe that she needed the OCD to get by; to make it. She is afraid that it is assisting her in correcting her previous mistakes and preventing her from making new ones.

Her perfectionism has pushed her to continue to be successful in many aspects of her life, despite her obstacles. She sometimes believes that her pain is what is assisting/helping her to become or remain the person she desires to be. She is haunted by what-if scenarios. What happens if she doesn't do it? What happens if she does this? What if she's just lying to herself? What if she further ruins her life by failing to control what she has the ability to control? Perhaps she can be whoever she wants if she continues to obsess.

"What are you thinking about?" the old woman asks.

"I don't know," she responds.

She chuckles, "You don't know, or you don't want to tell me?"

"I don't really want to tell you," she says with a grin.

"I see."

"Well also, it's complicated."

"Try me," the old woman says.

"It's more that I'm obsessing about everything that bothers me."

"You'll realize one day, perhaps when you are 40, that you are

wasting your time worrying about things. You have to let go, it's not healthy

to let yourself become consumed by your thoughts."

"I get that," she says, "but at the same time, I don't think it's

necessarily unhealthy. I can see the irrationality, but some of it I think is just

me needing and wanting to be the way I want to be."

She frequently uses analogies to explain her thoughts and beliefs to

others. One such analogy is the one about an athlete. An athlete, such as a swimmer training for the Olympics, allows his swimming to consume the majority of his time and energy. He spends countless hours training, eating for the body he needs in order to achieve his goals, obsesses over his wins and losses, and is tough on himself. After some time, let's say his doctor, therapist, friends, or someone close to him, convinces him that this is unhealthy; that he should focus on other things like relationships, other hobbies, and possible jobs. He begins to focus less and less on swimming. He never makes it to the Olympics because he is mediocre at everything. Years pass, and he is 70 or 80 years old when he realizes he made a mistake. Whether or not his obsessions were unhealthy, he should have continued to work toward becoming the person he desired to be, the person he is. He is now unable to return. It's all over.

The things she obsesses over may appear insignificant in comparison to a career, passion, or hobby, but she needs to be who she wants to be. She views herself as a piece of artwork, through her artistic eyes. The things she "needs" or tries to prevent, keep a certain way, or see, are all based on the fact that she doesn't assume or believe something bad will happen, but that she doesn't want to be seen, shown, or kept if it isn't polished the way she prefers.

This view can make others believe that she isn't trying. She is trying as hard as she can. Someone once said that she is drowning, but there is a floatie, and she isn't reaching for it. She sees the floatie, but it is in the shape of a shark fin. It could either be a floatie that can help her escape, or a shark ready to eat her alive; to destroy her.

Diamond

Under dense pressure,

does one crack,

sink lower,

or thrive?

Intensity, passion,

obsession,

fixation,

consumption.

A strong body still bleeds.

Inky salamander silk drips from

the heart like slip from

the limbs of sculpted muscles.

Polished zeal scratches

skin, extracts eyes,

carves tongues,

and burns organs.

Pressure of magnificence

can be blinding,

deafening, or

paralyzing.

You can be a diamond,

or you can turn to bones

like rattled skeletons

in the back of a closet.

Abating leads to deep regret.

It's too late to stop.

The colors are wet,

and the hunger has stained.

Rich obsession holds a lot of power; narrowing focus, freedom, and

time. A cracked sky of disgusting disorder and fixation can be blinding,

causing lower lips to involuntarily tremble under subconscious force. She

doesn't blame others for the entirety of her struggles. She knows she was

born with OCD, but others have contributed to her pain and distress. In the

past, she'd react to traumatic occurrences with a calm and collected

demeanor, before casually moving past them onto the next obstacle. As a hild, she'd go through phases, her focus shifting from one stressor or hread to another. After searching through her past to identify a cause or a 'why," she wound up with the burden of all versions of herself and all versions of her OCD. It's a lot of pressure. It's exhausting. It's worse at ight, for she wants to sleep, but her mind either won't let her, or she fears he inevitable reliving of past events. She doesn't sleep well anymore. Perhaps the lack of sleep is preventing her from having the arrant energy to piral as often as she used to. While she has had the power to avoid rabbit oles, she has yet to find the vanishing point of her intrusive plague of oughts.

She believes in certain things, and if those things are true, then her fe is ruined. She has said it over and over again; "If the things are not the ay I want them to be, if the things I believe are true, then I want to do erything in my power to make it the way I'd like." With the slim chance at things are the way she needs and have always been the way she wants, e is upset with those who have aided in the forming of her beliefs. She all not die clinging to grudges or postponed confessions of the tangible.

With pain, triggers, and the eliciting events, the origin of fear is pertinent and salient, but things that no person can rescind. Fixation can provide a sense of control or a false belief that somehow obsessing over the past can prevent further mistakes or shine a light on a reality other than OCD thoughts and pain.

In terms of communication and transmission, she prefers a telephoned touch of absence. She requires space or breaks from people and situations. Occasionally, what is spoken through a screen or through space is similar to what is spoken when unfiltered. Sometimes a form of barrier can release pressure, sometimes it can sever bonds, and other times, distance, with everything left in memory and one's mind, is better. Sometimes the distance or speaking only with distance, can make one feel connected or not alone, but take away the suffocation. She cares about people, but every once in a while, an escape is principled. She likes to be surrounded by people, without having to interact or communicate with them. One example of an escape is when she goes up to the cottage; a home away from the city. She isn't abandoning the ones she loves. She is just a phone call away. She requires a breather from the business, the pressure, and the stress. She decided to return to the cottage.

Through the dusted, webbed glass, she could see the bright green leaves, much more yellow and warm than the dark, rich green couch she is sitting on. As her eyes grew cross, her view of the warping window was interrupted by two beetles crawling up the aperture. Primitively, her eyes followed the crawling creatures, before rising to allow her feet to do the same. The bugs traveled along the edge of the floor, where the wood met the wall, and to the crack of the closet. Both beetles disappeared underneath the door, and for a moment, she paused.

She opens the door and lets her fingers fish through the clothing and boxes. Behind several faux-fur winter coats, she comes across a shoebox of letters. Her curiosity struck her, pushing her to open one of the envelopes. She unfolds the letter and grows more interested in the handwriting and expression, through the emotional text.

Through handwriting, one can presume an emotional state or tone through both the text itself, as well as the way in which the words are spaced, or attention to the quality of penmanship. The length of the letters, the size of the writing, and the pressure of the writing utensil all tell a story. Some are frustrated, some angry, some in pain, some sad, some cheerful, some exhausted, and some are too difficult to read.

Language, both written and spoken, is complex. She cares too much about saying the perfect thing; the right thing; the accurate thing. She wants her intentions to be clear. Oftentimes, memory or triggering speech can arouse rage, pain, or anxiety. Many conceal their true emotional state with every cell, and some think they are. Both concealing and attempting to conceal may reduce the human being to the skeleton filling their body to their core, or the snap peas of character, cased in intestinal gums; a human pod.

How easily can one decipher fear from anger, pain from strength, and happiness from lies? It depends on the wiring of one's brain. Words have a great deal of impact on any individual, weak or strong, young or old.

Miles away from everyone, years later, her mind is flooded with the individuals who have impacted her. Their sour words and punches had a strong influence on her. Do their knuckles ache? Her sores are becoming

increasingly difficult to heal, and her gashes are rejecting her stitches.

Her tongue swells with memories, begging to take the shape of a

strawberry in her throat. It's not all bad. Is it really that bad? Don't tell her

she's hysterical. It is not irrational to take the hit; to feel the hurt.

Which is the safer option; suppression, allowing leakage, or

accepting explosion? Why are people so damn defensive? Why aren't

people willing to admit their wrongs? She is beyond flawed, and she is

humble enough to admit it. She said she was ready for more. Is she? She

may be as fast as a peregrine falcon when fleeing, but she is also quickest

when showing up for someone. Where did everyone go? Did she push them

away, or did they leave on their own?

She felt as if the only thing she could cling to, to feel wanted or ok,

was the man who had violated her. That is grotesque. She despises him, but

she holds on to it. She holds onto something that has shot her down, because

the only person who had the power to change her view failed her. She is

aware that the person with the power should be herself, but it wasn't. She cannot remain in this dark cave. There is an escape, there is an out, there is an exit. She must find it. Perhaps she already has and is scared to use it.

She understands that she must leave behind every regret, every OCD belief, every painful experience, every sickening thought, and every person. She is all she is competent at being, and she must let go. She has been accepted and has committed to CSM for art in London. This relocation will serve as a fresh start for her. She has been to Trafalgar Square; the home of pigeons. Pigeons are both mysterious and abundant. She is well acquainted with them. She is familiar with the ones in New York City and San Francisco, and is getting to know the ones in London.

She may find new people to befriend or to form connections with. For the next person she is with, not that anyone will come along:

-She requires frequent space

-She is independent, but she is caring and kind

-She needs affirmation and quality time, but is not fond of physical touch

-She has a habit of pushing people away

-Her OCD can interfere with relationships and her attraction to others he has occasional panic attacks and depersonalization

ı addition to her passion for visual arts, she writes poetry, and

casionally sings

ler OCD is focused on appearance, contamination, something being just

ght, avoidance, relationships, and so forth

he was sexually assaulted at a young age

he is athletic and played sports, figure skated, rode horses, sung, and

ied

ler favorite place is her birthplace NYC

She loves traveling (explored 14-17 different countries)

he wants people to respect her boundaries

he is quiet and gentle, but opinionated

he is shy at first, taking a while to open up

he takes a lot of medication and has since she was a child

he wants to be loved, but she doesn't know if she has it in her anymore

She'll most likely scare everyone off. Sometimes she scares herself.

"I am the raven that rips myself apart endlessly. I have the power to let go. If I am a raven, I have given up flight; if I am a horse, I have given up running; if I am me, I shall move forward with grace."

Eagle

She has the power (or curse) to travel back in time, within her mind. She can place herself into her old body and take on or acquire former versions of herself. She can time travel into her past mindsets, personalities, and dressing styles, but she wants to escape. She feels as though nothing is real, nothing is right. The people around her say she is remarkable for getting through it, for her accomplishments. She was a baby bird and a child who wanted to be a beautiful woman, but now she wants to go back. She has attempted to erase the things that have happened, reverse the pain, and quiet the noise. She is disappearing, trying to look like the little girl she was with a BMI of 16.5, 16, standing under 96 lbs, turning to dust. She pushes through. She doesn't break. She will not break.

Animal

Your hands hugged my body,

fingers pet my waxen skin, puncturing my milky flesh.

You are heavy like a shire horse.

Oil hooves turned my ribs gray, and keratin tore tissue, exposing brittle

bones.

I've been slashed, stabbed, bitten, and bruised.

I've been harrowed and crucified but cased in elastic.

I waded through rivers of tart tears and black blood

as if muzzles weren't rusting my cheeks and my toes weren't tangled in

grease chains.

No, I won't let you rip me apart. I will bite back, I will fight,

and I will rise from the ground; the dirt that you tossed me upon.

I'm tethered to my past, but I will stitch myself back together.

Each bone, each crease, each scar, I am still me.

My fingers twitch as red leaks into the creases of my palm.

Colors mix with water like rinsed gouache.

I've been stripped naked in the soil, crumbling.

My limbs paralyzed, throat screaming, gut pulsating, stomach kissed,

body painted, nose leaking, and eyes draining.

I thought perhaps that meant I wasn't ugly.

I've failed to find 20 minutes of relief, distance from your flames.

I can't weaken your burn.

Drunken leeches suck venom from tender veins,

but you were an endoparasitoid that drained delicate arms for stolen

luminescence and luster. I don't sleep, I just dream. You did this to me.

I am not weak. You will not destroy me.

I try to go back to the little girl, but I can't.

The shade of my cheeks, the bones in my hand, the length of my hair,

the curve of my hips, the length of my frame,

the weight of my body, and the color of my lips, I wish to go back;

back to before you sprayed me like a skunk.

Your scent is always a cloud above my head, a ring around my neck.

Each letter and each word that trickled down your chin

are now bullets caught in my liver, stuck inside of me forever.

I can't ease the pain; the pain caused by coercion, caused by my fear,

by anguish, by her face, your words, my mistake.

I am the architect of my own cage, so I will escape.

She hopes that the four things she needs are the way that she needs

them to be (not the ugliest person, always thin, never disgusting, and not too

tan). She hopes that she is worthy, loved, that she is enough, that she didn't

ruin anything, that she will be happy, that what she wants will come to her,

and that she will be ok.

She views herself as a piece of artwork. Why would one exhibit an

unfinished, unpolished, ruined piece?

I am no masterpiece

I lather myself in silver,

sculpt my flaking flesh,

cut my discolored bones.

I trace my scars with graphite,

watercolor my bruises,

line my white skin with charcoal,

frame my blue-green eyes,

style my brown curls,

ce my red cheeks,

vet my red lips.

My body is destroyed

nd molded plant cellulose,

aud, dyes; paper clay paint.

am messy, chaotic,

isinterpreted, misshapen,

oorly painted, unpolished,

ith a pathetic surface,

aked with ink,

slapped with

thick strokes.

I cannot wipe the canvas clean.

I cannot make more clay.

It can't be undone.

There are no redos, only fixing.

One does not always

have the power

or control.

That leaves one solution;

to paint over,

add on, keep going.

The colors are too dark,

the material is too stubborn,

the surface is too torn to mend.

It; I am unfixable trash,

so why exhibit an unfinished,

ruined piece of artwork?

She almost fought it. She almost convinced herself it was deception; purely a mind's trick. Several friends and strangers have assured her that her obsessions, compulsions, and her reactions were all just OCD; all false. Even her father told her that she was always thin, that she was never disgusting or ugly. She needed to hear that, but she needed the reassurance and the words from those who contributed to the inflammation or seed of those obsessions. Her mother never gave her a response to panic that could convince her that it was just in her head, therefore, she confirmed her beliefs. She didn't want to fight the truth, for that meant she would be lying to herself, gliding through life as purely, stupidly unaware of the mistakes she has or would make. She needed to make sure everything was perfect from now on. No more mistakes, for she already ruined her life. For her, it had to be always, or it didn't satisfy her or "count."

It's all wasted; her life, her energy, her time, everything is wasted. It shouldn't have had to be like this. Why couldn't she enjoy her life?

She is strong. She is independent. She doesn't need anyone, but she doesn't want to be completely alone. She just requires a lot of space. She is complex. She wants to fight for her happiness.

Tit

layhouse

wicker and time.

ike a widow with wine,

'll cut the sun

om the sky,

or dark is warm

the crisp

nd cold in heat.

Darkness is not absence,

ut simply

hat isn't.

It is as if

one is attempting

to locate

their head,

chasing after their mind

in faint light,

or searching

for a card

of diamonds

amongst a thousand hearts.

This is comparable

to digging for the

gold of happiness.

Each person's strength,

their darkness,

and struggle.

Their future is

lapidarian, but

their future is not written.

Their graven

bodies and minds

are merely warned

by a caution tape for action.

The rules have

been printed,

roles approved,

values decided,

deeds have been made,

and the clock is ticking

in the playhouse

of design.

like a child

playing school,

playing family,

playing house,

pretending,

or acting,

the imagined is often

a child's act for fun.

They act as if

they are strong;

strong enough

to tame a lion,

and if not,

then a cock.

As people age,

some continue to act.

They choose the pretend,

embody another,

express that pain

without anyone

knowing it's theirs.

We are impregnated

with fear, with sorrow,

with sin, bloated

like a balloon tied to a roof.

The pretending;

the playing house;

the elegant accord and

desolate interior

of all the pieces

that hide childish dreams.

It's ironic,

for the beautiful

had become

plain and smaller.

Erasures and disguise

both make one

utterly worn out.

It's the purist caprice

with white boxes

of apprehension

and security.

Cadences,

vague speech,

fixed bleakness,

pale pleasure,

reverse grimace

in absolute mourning,

and gauzy veils

make humans

cotton pawns.

This is a playhouse;

a child's or an adult's.

We eat, we drink,

we sleep, we dream,

we work, we cry,

we laugh, we speak,

we live, and we die.

We die like the sun

as it is cut from the sky.

It is cut from the sky

and pasted on the floor

of a playhouse.

Instantaneously, as if the train is lined with vats of perfume, ripe fragrances kiss the hairs against her arm. She scrunches her nose and rotates, facing away from the skunk's direction. As her head pivots, she meets the eyes of the old woman. The old woman had placed her book away and, in its place, the cheeks of The New Yorker are pinched by her shriveled fingers.

"Excuse me," the old woman says, with a puny tremor in her voice.

"Yes?"

"What is a 10-letter word for sociable?"

"Extroverted," says a man with a bird tattooed on his neck.

She finds herself gazing at his tattoos for a minute too long. Her eyes follow the trail from his neck to the web and spider branded on his ear.

"No, dear," she responds.

After the distraction, she answers. "Gregarious," she says.

"Clever girl."

She gazes over at the tattooed man once again. He meets her eyes with eyes sharper than any she has seen before. She didn't think that was possible. She can feel the palpitations in her chest and her blotched neck.

He winks, and though he is gorgeous, with butterfly-stained scleras and arper than a knife, no set of eyes can rival blueberry paragon. She will

ver allow him to fade. She hopes he doesn't let her fade.

The burden of mistake, imperfection, of regret, and of sempiternal

e are heavy, like a plaster foot tied around her ankle, like intestines

gging the wooden floor, like snapped wishbones, like white body bags in

grass, like a hammer hammering itself, like scissors cutting themselves,

like her hands strangling her own neck.

Before her mind guides her through one of those scenarios, the

bway voice announces the next stop, as a gentleman with a ducktail beard

d a multi-shade, blue shirt (that resembles walls of a floral-themed

mmer home) squeezes through the closing doors. The shirt is a white and

ie button-down, with tiny flowers. The pattern reminded her of a covering

one of the second-floor bedrooms in the cottage she occasionally visits.

She begins to feel her skirt dirtied by the damp grass; soft green

ae tentacles of the land. The dirt turns to mud from the heavy east coast

n. She can almost feel the water twirling around the follicles of hair on

r arm when she notices a familiar face; a face she cannot name. She glances periodically in their direction, attempting to recall where she

recognizes them from.

Four women begin to speak loud enough for anyone on the train t

hear.

One woman asks, "What about the one with the lace?"

"No, I don't like lace."

"Ok," she says.

"I thought the cream one was beautiful," another exclaims.

The bride-to-be begins to speak, "It was gorgeous, but..."

"I thought you looked like a queen."

"But I don't want to look like a queen."

"What about the last one you tried on?"

"It's not tight and small enough," she says.

"You don't want it to be too revealing."

"Yeah, but I want him to think I look sexy, not slutty, but sexy."

"You can look sexy in all of them," her mother says.

"He likes tight ones."

"Ohhh, ok, he's one of those."

"What? He doesn't even like it when I wear a flowy mini dress. He was like, mmm, maybe you should put something else on."

"Wow, he's opinionated."

"Yeah."

"So let's keep looking," the mother says.

She felt herself growing warmer and cooler at the same time. She feels as she does in a state of high anxiety or when she is uncomfortable, with heat in her cheeks and a sharp pinch at her hip. She goes back to the burning.

Burning

She is

Burning,

In pain,

On fire,

In the fire,

Burning,

Out of the fire,

In the water,

In the ocean,

In the sea,

Swimming,

Drowning,

Wanting to

Be burning.

She has to

Let go

Or she'll burn

Or drown,

But if she does,

Her entire world

Will disappear

And wash up

On black

Burnt sand.

But what now?

Maybe she

Should

Just sit in

A puddle

Of urine;

Sit and let

Her body

Rot,

Her veins

Swell, and

Her flesh prune

In the uncomfortable

Reek of

Warm piss.

It is worse

Than tears,

Than spit,

Than coming.

She'd be like

A shivering

Wick sitting

In wax.

The lights

Are shot.

Blow her out.

Make it

All go dark.

She is

Letting go.

It's all

Too heavy;

Too heavy

For her bleeding,

Bruising body.

No.

Fuck no.

She's not

Giving up.

She'll rip

The weak

blobs from

between

silicone legs.

She'll bite

your motherfucking

tongue and

Make it bleed.

She is strong.

She is no longer

A silenced shadow,

No longer

Rattled bone.

Fight her.

Somehow, she, a woman, repeatedly winds up feeling helpless,

naked, and cold.

She drank blood for warmth and strength, but it seems as though the

blood drank her.

The disrespect towards women almost makes no sense, for a woman

is the source of a man's very breath. Men disrespect her. People disrespect

her. They don't listen. They push. They force. They manipulate. They

ignore. They provoke. They trigger. People can be rotten; rotten like the

chemicals that drink her freedom. They are foul like rows of leather diseas like a virus. Once you are infected; once you are aware of something, you will never be able to fully change your thinking or to entirely forget. It is a virus; a virus that can be self-created or one that can be affected by others. It can spread within one person's body or pass on with every kiss, every handshake, everything one touches, in food, and in the air inhaled and exhaled. Like any child, any baby, any person at all, there are things she needs.

Beaks Break

Beaks break

branches and twigs

like an umbilical

cord is cut.

Blood twigs and leaves

are crimson

like the

ink tattooed

by a mother

to a daughter,

into her veins.

A brood,

a clutch

of feathers,

mouth stretched

open and wide,

await the

food and nutrients

to help them

grow and flourish.

They sit in

the nest,

he mother

eeding them.

They wait,

mouth stretched,

aces open and wide,

waiting for what

hey need;

what they ache for.

They open their mouths,

knowing they will not

be fed what they want to be fed.

They open their mouths anyway.

Now their mouths drip red as the

ops of their heads tilt back.

heir feathers and necks

oint at the sun;

a blood-red sun.

She is the blood-red sun.

She should be the warm,

comforting sun.

She is the hot,

burning sun.

     She is not lost or allowing herself to waste away. She is seeking

freedom and ways to mend her fractured self-perception. Her body is like a

deep, dark, cold body of water. Her teeth are bluish, her legs detached. Her

hands, her neck, her thighs were ice, but her chest, her stomach, and her

face were hot. She can no longer see nor hear. She is clouded with a shy

silence; subdued language.

     Beneath the surface, many creatures, numerous shards, and

fragments of past versions of herself are embedded under glass, at the

bottom. The weight of her triggers, the memories, the associations that

change her mindset, her views, her obsessions, and compulsions drag her wn.

A person, a place, an object, a smell, a taste, anything can trigger a
ange in view for her. She absorbs the mindset of a time that the trigger
ninds her of. She feels as though she is caught in the past, and she can
apse in terms of old habits or regain old symptoms of her OCD. This shift
not usually voluntary. She cannot choose, making it difficult for her to
nain in the present.

She feels boneless, soggy, and twisted, with a shapeless blood
erior. She attempts to protect herself and her heart through the whittling
her stone exterior; a layer built around her broken ribs. She is either
eltering or trapping herself. She is either keeping the air in or imprisoning
rself by holding breaths of misery captive. Every breath she takes feels as
ough she is facing death. She is a delicate ghost, her body a surreal
ment, her mind lapping beyond control. She isn't hollow, but her inside
ho places of emptiness and hunger. Specks of fulfillment, satisfaction, and
od fill her organs with punctured holes; holes with ribbons running
ough them, tying her to her past and to her triggers. She is hungry for

relief, for ease, for something to help her, or even just a taste of freedom.

Bottle

Hungry

Hungry

Feed me

Please feed me

Don't feed my obsession

Don't feed my compulsions

Don't feed my delusion

Feed me strength

Feed me the truth

Feed me acceptance

Feed me hope

Feed me something other than pain

Bottle

There's a bottle

of her

mother's love

sitting on the

kitchen table.

It's spoiled.

It had to be

kept in

the fridge.

She left it out.

It's gone bad.

Time to toss

out.

It isn't

sour milk.

Instead of

pouring the liquid

down the drain,

she put

flowers in

the bottle's throat,

hoping to

revive them.

The flowers were then

poisoned by the

spoiled love.

The flowers are

ow flowers of evil.

he bottle

f love is no

onger a bottle of love.

t is a bottle

f pain;

bottle

f lacking,

f wanting.

Guillemot

Goth:

Black sky

Green earth

Brown dirt

Purple bones

Silver eyes

Silver fingers

Green shirt

Leather jacket

Black shirt

Black skirt

Black dress

Brown dress

Brown hair

Red cheeks

Red lips

Purple skirt

Purple rings

Black mascara

Fair skin

No sun, no light

Cold flesh

Black blood

Red heart

All dark

No reflection

Nocturnal

Sharp teeth

Vampire?

She wants to escape. She wants to be free. She knows who she is
and what she wants. She just loses sight of complete reality at times. She
sees the world as entirely black and white. She wants things to be black and
white. She wants all or nothing. She likes certainty. It is either the pain of
what is divergent from what she needs or the burn of being chewed from the
inside without knowing. Not knowing is intolerable, like solidified blood.

She was the golden child and could hide her pain, but now she is
silver. She is exhausted; tired of both the hiding and of her routine. She is
worn out and drained of every last drop of energy. She is tired of the
showers and the late-night compulsions. She is tired of the fear. God, she

wants to sleep. The exhaustion is weakening her brain. She is tired of the interior focus; the vivid contradictions of logical and illogical, whether a world parallel to the outside one or completely irrational, with no overlap with the exterior life. She just wants to be ok, she wants to be pretty, to be clean, to be kind, to be accepted. Like pimples that wash away, like the sea comes and goes, like the sun comes and goes, like people come and go, her ability to focus on what is truly important is not a constant.

She wishes she could tolerate more. She wishes her body, mind, and heart weren't so sensitive. She wishes the words of someone she had only known for a few weeks hadn't robbed her of the 0.1 percent of hope she had left. He stole it from her with phrases that taught her that she was correct. She was right to be in pain, unhappy, paranoid, and paralyzed. She can't fight what shouldn't be fought. She desires and deserves the pain. She has completely ruined everything. She thought she'd fixed the present and was focusing on the fact that she couldn't change the past, but now she realizes that the current version of herself isn't who she wants to be.

She has no control over anything she does anymore. She has no control over how others perceive her. When she says no, they don't listen.

She says no, which causes others to try to persuade or manipulate her into

agreeing, doing, or saying what they want. People don't listen when she tell

them to resist doing something, and they get angry when she tells them to

be vigilant or to attempt to comprehend.

It's ludicrous because even if she simply requests that someone stop

saying something, she is the dramatic one; the one who asks for too much

when all she wants is for someone to care enough to be cautious around her

An act of kindness; an act of service, similar to how she expresses

and communicates her love. Others' love languages may include touch, gift

giving, words of affirmation, and so on, but hers are quality time and acts o

service. She deserves someone who cares enough to check in, rather than

acting as if she should just keep everything inside and stay silent. She is on

constant alert for the event of someone she knows or cares about

interpreting an action or comment in a way that could affect them, as some

occurrences have affected her. She doesn't want anyone to feel as she does.

She is gracious, polite, and considerate. She cares. She presumes others do ɔt. They have the impression that she doesn't. She used to prioritize

veryone, and she still does a significant portion of the time. Some say she

ɔts as if she doesn't care. It's fascinating because she'd argue that they don't

ɪre either. Everyone has a different love language.

Hers is characterized by acts of service and quality time. It appears

ɔ though she doesn't care because she isn't physically or verbally

ffectionate on a regular basis. She is sensitive, she listens to people, she

ɔaches out, checks in, and spends time with those she cares about. People

ɪrely listen to her, respect her, or even attempt to understand her. They

ɪsmiss, downplay, forget, or simply lack concern.

Every romantic encounter, every friend, relative, and even stranger

ɪe speaks with, doesn't seem to love like she does. They are concerned, but

ɔt on a comparable level. She would tear herself to shreds for the sake of

thers. She can't let go, and she never will. It tarnishes and breaks her heart

ɔ leave, to be left, to try to forget, to change, and to move on. She simply

ants to feel understood, as if her concept of love can be matched; the

rength, degree, wave of love, respect, and adoration.

Due to her overthinking, she can't always figure out what she wants or how she feels about something. When she is asked to provide an answer or make a decision, her brain automatically considers the options, preventing her from determining how she feels or which of the options she prefers. She knows what she wants at times, but she also knows that she must consider what she needs and which of the options is best for both her and others.

Her brain enjoys trickery, games, and manipulation. It manipulates her through causing her to doubt her instincts, to focus on the wrong things; the corporeal, right from wrong, perfect and imperfect, and preventing ruin or regret.

Toxic-Escape

OCD and I are two stalkers, stalking each other in love.

Neither of us will give up, we can't get enough.

We're so compelled, it's blinding.

You're so compelled to never let me be,

and I, to never let go; to let go of

what is protecting me, loving me.

know you think the same as me, but I have control.

am simply choosing to give you the reins.

Perhaps you have manipulated me into doing so.

Is this familial or institutional? Is this me or a disease?

This crippling fear is tap, tap, tapping on my ribs,

leaving bruises. The marks are reminders; triggers.

You expose yourself. You expose me.

lie languid, consciously or unconsciously glassy and spectral.

The bruises color my torso just below my heart;

just below a heart that is half yours.

gave you a piece of my heart. No, you stole it.

That is love, I suppose.

Let me bask in the torture.

I was once rough and clear with beautiful holes.

My exterior is now smooth like a

well-worn piece of glass.

My own hallowed body is dragging me

through shards and fragments, through memories.

I followed you, I listened, I obeyed,

throwing my thin, tired body.

Another me, inside my body is dragging

me into bodies of water, within bodies of water.

The water is colder, darker, and deeper than

any body of water or the deepest depth of the sea.

This is a sea of lovers;

a sea where people

get lost in the push

nd pull of affection, attention,

fatuation, admiration, acceptance,

erfection, life, love, reality, and not.

he line between reality and imaginary

  similar in thickness

 the line between life and art.

's similar to my art

raxis and practice.

should allow for a loss of control.

Vhen considering corporeal focuses,

must give up control over a viewer or person's perception.

give your perception too much power.

ly meticulous attempts to be

specific way dominates me.

hey dominate me like you do.

They take my freedom as you do.

Though you have stolen my ability to think freely, I still choose you. Why?

Is it due to safety and comfort?

This is not comfortable. Where is my bravery?

I know I have to let go,

but you must let go too.

Let go of your rigid control and provide me

with an openness and blankness.

The complexities of our love

are overwhelming and confusing.

I feel misguided.

Why don't we fight?

At least let it be subconscious or subtle, or intense and implemented,

to capture the contrast between realism and irrational.

m too intimate and quiet.

his is practically a vexed relationship.

ou have confused my relationship

etween the psyche and people or place.

am blind in love. At first, you stalked me,

ut now I stalk you when I feel you fading.

She attempts to share the constant toxic relationship between her

CD and herself. As she shares her experiences and pain, she feels as

ough she is acting and appearing self-centered. Should she back off?

hould she keep quiet?

How can she when there is constant torment and discomfort? There

something wrong with her body. There is something wrong with her.

veryone else is perfect. She feels herself slipping. She needs certainty,

tensity, and for everything to be worth her time. Like linoleum relief, she

arves and carves bits of herself away. Unlike cutting linoleum, she doesn't

et to choose what remains and what is visible. She doesn't have enough control. She needs control. She is considering the phenomenological.

She is challenging and questioning her perceptions and accepted "truths," whether proven correct or incorrect. She is discovering realities and pondering the ephemeral. Her maturity and insight have allowed for her to analyze the dialogue between internal and external, as well as the friction between cognitive perceptions, dreams, and subtle failures, that distinguish what is real and what is not. Is the retroflection positive or negative? She is attempting to figure out if keeping the OCD by her side is helping her, or solely a source of pain. She is waiting until she is ready to tackle.

The truth is, her OCD would be nothing without her. It needs her as a subject to control. It's almost as if the relationship mirrors the relationship between a plant and water. Sometimes she feels like the flower and the OCD is the water, allowing her to bloom and flourish. Sometimes she is like the water. She waters the OCD, allowing it to grow. She has to let the plant die.

Her mind is slapped with the awareness of the woman holding her phone at an angle. She cannot tell if she is taking a photograph or holding r phone oddly. A consequential aggregation of time is spent on

elioration of herself and her virtues. She can't take the risk. Although the

in is swaying aggressively, she rises and rushes to a different seat. She

solutely abhors photographs. Photos of herself inflict so much pain and

comfort, that she begins to obsess and panic over their existence. The

rpose of a photograph is the exact reason she loathes them. She is utterly

ulsed by her appearance and the pressure of documenting the superlative,

cise moment. An entirely accurate photo of an individual does not exist.

erefore, if a photo is for memory or documentation, she doesn't want that

age to be how she is perceived. She has requested that every photograph

en of her in the past has been deleted, and she refuses to take any in the

sent or future. The photo never goes away; it never disappears. A

otograph is taken to capture one's appearance, document physical

anges, aging, legacy, and practically making us immortal. If a photo is

en for control, why does it feel like the lack of it? People have a

cination with personal perception through others' lenses. We, as humans,

ve an inherent desire to see how we look.

Unfortunately, for her, the timeframe she lives in is the digital age. If she could have existed in the past, it would erase a significant portion of her constant pain. She doesn't want a photo to be how she is remembered. She doesn't want her face, her body, her clothing, her hair, or any part of her to be captured by a phone or a camera. She prefers to hide from a lens. If one sees an image of something, one will assume that is how it looks. If one sees a picture of a relative as a child, they will have no idea what they truly looked like in person, because they weren't present at that moment of time. The only thing one has as reference to how one looked is the knowledge they have; the photograph. One's face is a vulnerable presentation of oneself. Vulnerability, discomfort, ugliness, beauty, strength, weakness, and flaws are blended into the pixels of a face.

Documentation is not reality. A photo alters the appearance of a person, object, or place. The angle, the aesthetic, the focus, and the composition all contribute to the altering of reality. There is practically a conspiracy with the taking of a photo and the camera. In addition to inaccurate recording and representation of an object, the images can now be lited and altered digitally. She would go back and prevent herself from

/er taking a photo. There is friction between what is mandatory and what

avoidable or voluntary. Government-mandated images, proof of

:istence? What if it is avoidable? Can one escape it?

Everyone has traits, character, a body, a mind, emotions, and likes

ıd dislikes, therefore their opposite or alternate exists within possibility. A

:rson is formed by their genetics, their brain functionality, their

ıowledge, and awareness. If one instance is shifted slightly by the smallest

itervention, it can warp and alter one's current state of being. She has an

ternate self. Her OCD is a major part of her life. When she gives it

ıntrol, it can form everything. What if she didn't have it? What would she

ok like, act like, sound like, think like?

ower Of Pain

ıe takes

:e world's pain

as her own pain,

in addition to

her own pain.

She takes

the pain

reflexively.

Torment hides

in her eyes

and in the

palpitations of

her heart.

She didn't know

her hands held

so much strength.

She didn't

realize that

she was capable

of biting

as she was bitten.

She wants

to save people,

not hurt people.

Did they want

to save her

or hurt her?

Look at the

mess made.

It's the game

they've played.

There were

no winners;

both losers.

Now they don't

have to play,

for one forfeit,

and when they

repealed their decision,

the other one withdrew.

Perhaps they are happy.

Perhaps they don't

care about winning,

only that the other loses.

A dog whines, and the old woman folds her stomach over her knees

and she scratches its chin. The dog tilts its head back as she says, "Do you

like the train, sweet boy?"

"Her name is Beatrice."

"Oh, I'm sorry, sweet girl, "the old woman says.

She shifts her eye from the woman, to the owner, to the dog, and

back to the owner. All she can think about is a dog with a bone.

ne

u are the dog.

ave a bone.

rhaps I

the dog.

u are

owner.

ave a bone.

eep burying

d retrieving

bone;

one

m a ghost

neath the dirt.

vas

ombination

of hide-and-seek

and fetch.

It was more

complex than

the average game.

I abandoned the game.

You played until you

got tired,

until we

were both ghosts.

I was the ghost first.

Now you

don't reply,

but you'll always

be my favorite ghost.

God-damn

it hurts.

ou were right.

he obsession

asn't

y reason of

rst love.

othing compares.

the wake

f persistent ache,

y ribs and tissues

rt like mountains

vealing a valley

d a sea.

slid down

the sea.

slid from

e mountains,

eeding through

my fingers,

clutching a

treasure in

my hands.

A treasure;

a heart;

something I

thought I left

In my room,

In seattle,

In your dorm,

In my dorm,

In basement

practice rooms,

and gender-neutral

bathrooms,

and couches,

and the cabin,

In the patch of skin

on my cheek,

In the kisses,

In eyes,

In freckles,

In the ash.

Everything

I thought I knew

is dust.

I wasn't everything.

I don't have

anything left

to give.

I would commit

in a second,

without hesitation.

I know there

is no use

trying anymore.

I respect

your wish.

I won't text,

I won't call,

I won't write.

I'll only dream.

I buried

the compulsions

like a bone.

It is taking

every muscle

in my body

to have restraint;

to leave

bone

the dirt;

leave

hidden

tween a

nga of sticks,

den in the dirt,

den like a bone.

Swan

Re-soiling is essentially like refilling or possibly emptying eye

sockets. It's both positive and negative, comforting and uncomfortable.

When one looks back on humiliating delicacy, they notice their ignorance

the presence of mass beasts amid darkness.

She has sat on many mattresses that have whispered secrets of blue

violation, of hypnotism, of unripe sunny days, of faded torsos, of trust, of

blue gardens, and mountains of memory, amplified cries of tension, dented

disorder, and nervous purple grayness.

She must let go. Is it better to let go and fly away, or to stay put?

What demonstrates more strength? Though her pain may appear dramatize

or self-inflicted, she is unlike many in terms of self-help. She is doing the

work. She has tried numerous medications and a multitude of therapies,

working hard on her exposure tasks and improvement plans. She has established an exposure hierarchy and is addressing each type of compulsion, one at a time. She's refrained, altered, and performed. Her anxiety levels have not decreased, nor have they increased.

As she fingers the tension-angered, swollen patch of skin between her left eye and ear, her phone blinks and light radiates. The man beside her glances down at her flickering phone. "Screenpeeker;" she thinks to herself as she rolls her eyes slightly. As she reads the notification, it says, "There is only so much strain that your heart can handle. Why are you holding on to something that isn't coming back?"

Her mind commanded him to let her go. She didn't want it. She did and didn't at the same time. Periodically, she thinks about what she would say. "If you let go, just know, I never will, I never can, I never want to. I'll it with the pain. I choose to let myself think of you. I don't beg my brain to orget. I allow the thoughts to pile up, to dance with me every day. You robably fell in love again. I know that I won't find what I thought I had ith you again. Whatever this does, don't let it let you tell me that you don't ve me anymore. He basically said it was all a lie. Let me pretend. Let me try?"

She isn't going to hold as tightly, though. She is loosening her grip on the past. Did she make a mistake about the man after? Is she really asking for too much?

Is she confusing obsession and intensity with love? The one after had the audacity to say he loved her when he failed to accept her as the individual she is. One cannot; one does not get to say "I love you," if one does not actually want the individual. How could a man say he loves a woman if he believes she is asking for too much, if he can't understand her, and if he doesn't see her for her worth? He is a good man, just not the right man. It doesn't matter how little she knew him or how little he knew her, the fact that he saw her as a bigger person and a tan person, despite her hiding her skin and her weighing 95 pounds as a 5'4 woman, just confirmed her OCD beliefs. She'll never relax. He wasn't the right man. He can't be right, right? He is just a man.

He is a man that told her to refine her definition of happiness. Her standards are so low, that her definition cannot be more reasonable. Her ide of happiness is simply just twenty minutes pain-free; twenty minutes of breathing without strain; twenty minutes without feeling like she is burning or drowning. How can one truly be a happy person if they have loved, or if they have been broken.

If his idea of love is what he claims love to be, then he has never felt and never known real, genuine, true love. Her love is se-eternal. He can't say he loves her, for if he does, he is stripping the word of its meaning, allowing for the possibility that when the people she believed had said that phrase, that they too, could have meant it as a tangible, disposable thing. Love is forevermore; love doesn't die. A person can be gone, but the love, he love, or at least the love she feels, is immortal. She, like everyone else, deserves a great love. One that is great, not perfect. Nothing can be perfect. She is tired, weary of the weight she's been holding. She must leave what's heavy behind. She doesn't get lonely. She likes solitude, but sometimes, she thinks about the absence of love.

She is laying her weapons down. Her heart breaks for the world. Once she cares, she never stops. It is like people are oceans, and she is trying to find out how deep their water goes. Is it only as deep as she can see? People return, but can they remain, or are they like rain? Is she still a rain keeper, or has she lost every last drop of control?

Her head and neck feel as though they are made of granite. She scratches her flaking, dry neck. She goes back again. It's almost as if her thoughts are light switches. One thought is turned off and the second pressure pulls or pushes the switch up or down, a new thought pops up, or an old one returns.

She returns to the negativity; images of her dry neck, like her dry hands, her dry lips, like cracked lotion, like cracked lube, like vanilla, like the vanilla that coated her, moisturizing her skin. Vanilla, once her favorite scent, reeks of bacteria, and of repulsion. She must snap out of it. It's hard to shift one's focus when pain sucks all comfort, all clarity, all oxygen.

She must look for another smell. There is a man who smells like bathroom hand soap. There is another man holding his wrists as if they are in cuffs; as if he is guilty of something. As he shakes his legs, he eyes a woman wearing all black, except for her red Mary Janes. She is scarfing a croissant, as its crumbs cling to her sweater. She couldn't help but let her eyes connect the crumbs like a "connect-the-dots" or constellations. The rain comes to a halt and the woman stands to exit at her stop. The crumbs fall to the ground, leading her eye to an unattended parcel on the ground. Then goes her wandering mind. It's like a drinker who keeps taking another drink. She becomes engulfed in an imagined reality; a still life, but one full of movement. The parcel becomes whatever she imagines it to be. It's as if 's an alternate reality, but those realities, they tell her about her truth and her desires. It's as if she is on a river afloat, immobile on a wilted mattress; mattress on which her mind relapses. Her thoughts and emotions are most viral, and if so, then the infection has spread too far and deep. It is a part of her. While removed, nevertheless, she is highly functional. She can manage.

Her frame feels heavy and inflexible, like gray rest, under strange sunlight. She hides her pink cheeks like a vampire squid, and she rubs her fleshless bits in hopes that she'll disappear. Her insides need scraping like expression of flesh. Her synthetic demeanor is like vascular skin and tufted fabric.

Velvet

Teased features,

Fallen follicles,

Leather shoulders,

Black cotton,

Purple mesh,

Orange silk,

Red Velvet,

Velvet like mornings,

Velvet nights,

Velvet dreams.

She is merely

a robust individual

nidst a crisis,

1asing strength

frighten dogs

1d reduce

nsions of

ease-stained dialect

1oken from eroded lips

a frenetic mind.

:itches that cross

purple-punched spine

1 a porcelain back

ust be widened

reveal damp,

1sfiguring irrationality.

he lurks in a courtyard

f planted fantasy,

amateur to the confrontation

of the difficulties of flushed age.

The cold ferocity chokes

strangers who wipe

her soaked red face

and finger her rose-ringed neck.

Translucent skin sheds like a white moth.

Her skeleton continues

to be trailed; a tracing that will be done

over and over like fingers on a lover's skin,

the tracing occasionally

limited to one's mind.

Guiding Outlines

are collapsed to become softer

like the bloodiest

roars yielding

to a splintered sky.

There is an

exchange of thinking.

It is as if each lavender freckle;

glitter on her arms

beget an optical or haptic gaze.

One suggests

distance and perspective

to survey and categorize.

It is associated with

clarity and reason,

organizing the world,

and the other

collapses distance

and blurs the familiar

through intimacy.

Figures are bedizened to match

the prevalent like stripped petals.

They stand naked as the epicalyx

is plucked when ardent

disposition is no longer young.

Contamination of change, growth,

and decay licks lips and tickles the stomachs of birds,

a harsh inevitable like the pressure of lungs

on a rib cage as one expands

like magma under a ceiling of knives.

The knives are clean, though;

no blood, no skin, no wings;

a relaxed presentation of a haunting paralyzation.

Each being is crushed to the height

of potential and restraint.

A crumpled, torn structure of beauty

remains in a world of strange frequencies,

shiny flickers of glamor, and tactile illusions.

Her burdening attire is made of silver,

soldering her thoughts and mind to her figure.

She seeks a balance;

harmony; no cancellation;

frame supporting and

holding memory, the real,

the imagined, the quiet,

the ghosts, and the games.

She sits like a silver-painted

porcelain doll,

suffocated with

velvet silk.

She almost fought it. She almost convinced herself it was deception purely a mind's trick. Several friends and strangers have assured her that her obsessions, compulsions, and her reactions were just OCD; all false. Even her father told her that she was always thin, that she was never disgusting or ugly. She needed to hear that, but she needed the reassurance and the word from those who contributed to the inflammation or seed of those obsessions. Her mother never gave her a response to panic that could convince her that it was just in her head, therefore, she confirmed her beliefs. She didn't want to fight the truth, for that meant she would be lying to herself and glide through life as purely, stupidly unaware of the mistakes she has or would make. She needs to make sure everything is perfect from now on. No more mistakes, for she already ruined her life. For her, it had to be always, or didn't satisfy her or "count." Despite the hardships, she will take the blame. She has made too many mistakes. She is staunch, for she aches to reach perfection, for the cessation of horrid legacies, to fix everything, and make everyone happy.

She thought she was a rainkeeper; one who could wash away t

oken shells, the trash, the dirt, the negative; one who could hold in her

ars and water the struggling stems and seeds around her, but she is not a

inkeeper, for the OCD has taken over, and it is washing the world away.

It's the second rush hour now, and the subway is flooded with late-

ght commuters. She observes the individuals practically hugging each

her. Their dewy arms kiss the poles and foggy reflective doors. She

udies a middle-aged man clutching his valise. The bend of his briefcase

adges at the tired old woman's side.

"Excuse me," she says softly,

"Yes?"

"You should probably rest your briefcase somewhere else."

"Why?"

"I know it's crowded, and we are crunched, but you could turn it on

s side," she says.

"He squints."

"It's touching the woman," she says.

"What woman?" he asks.

"The one to your left that the corner of your bag is against."

"There is no one there."

The train stops once again. It's the last train, and everyone exits th subway. She inhales deeply, shutting her eyes. She hugs her body, cold i the humidity. Her sun is ice, like a swan who slept too long, in a freezir lake. Her feet are light on the thick, yellow platform line. The souls of he shoes prevent her from experiencing the haptic qualities of the smal protruding bellies swelling from the yellow surface. She spins to watch th train leave the station. As the last car passes, it reveals the object on th tracks. Lying there, on the tracks, are feathers and a bloody beak. flattened, shivering bird lies on the cold, black earth. It's time to fly, eve when wings have been clipped. She craves the still, but she needs to mov She is only a cygnet. She is young. She was young.

Acknowledgments

The events, people, and belief system are all true. The individuals included in the book, additional relatives, past and present friends, roommates, and several arts and writing teachers have significantly influenced my work and growth as an artist, a writer, and a young woman.

Contact Information

Email: Olivia.walker@interlochen.org
Email: oliviaart.walker@gmail.com

Please refrain from commenting on the specific OCD beliefs, for opinions are adverse.

Bio Replication

Olivia Walker is a visual artist and writer, born in New York City and raised predominantly in California. Her work portrays her experience with OCD, and her practice has aided her in finding solace. She has learned to embrace the positive qualities that stem from the diagnosis. In her writing; her narrative of scene and summary, her poetry, and complex literary pieces, she considers and addresses a multitude of struggles: obsessions, compulsions, triggers, and depersonalization/derealization that come with OCD. She strives to find the balance between the grotesque and beautiful and discomfort and solace.

She investigates the dialogue and dichotomy between intimacy and opposition, structure and ruin, reality and unreality, and inner battles with order and chaos. She hopes her intricate, picturesque, vulnerable, metaphorical, and insightful writing can act as exposure and a tool for moving on, accepting, and escaping her past, as well as a platform to de-stigmatize mental illness.

CPSIA information can be obtained
at www.ICGtesting.com
Printed in the USA
LVHW061342090723
751696LV00010B/212